ITS BEAUTIFUL HERE

MEGAN MORTON

captured by

Brooke Holm

Thames & Hudson

Audacity.

Find it,

use it,

abuse it.

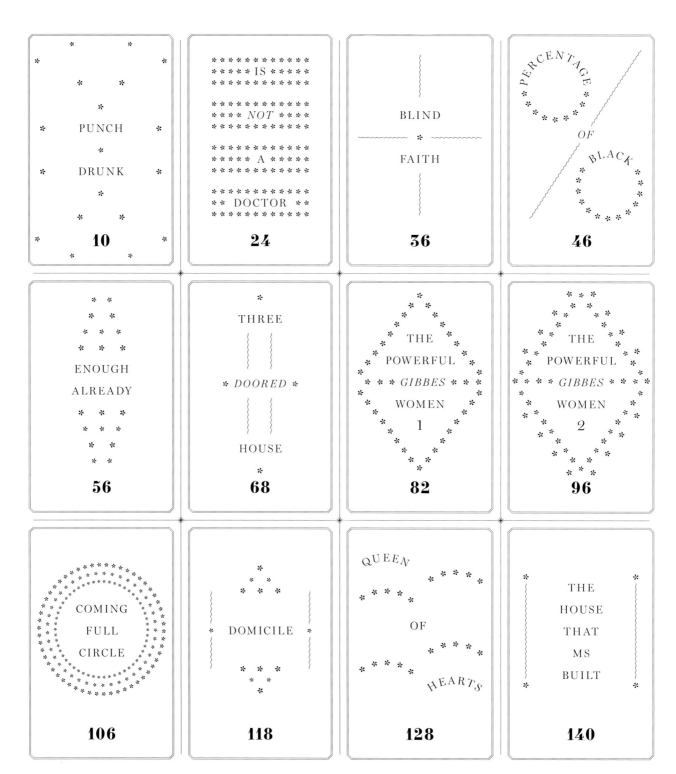

THERE IS
SOMETHING ABOUT

```
      *
    * H *
    * A *
      *
    * N *
      *
    * Y *
      *
    * A *
      *
```

150

G E N E T I C

G I F T S

162

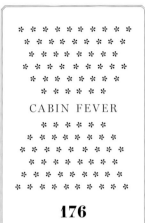

CABIN FEVER

176

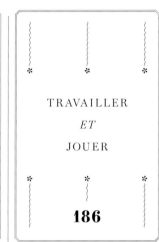

TRAVAILLER
ET
JOUER

186

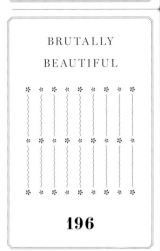

BRUTALLY
BEAUTIFUL

196

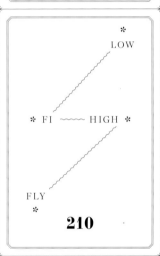

LOW

FI — HIGH

FLY

210

THE HOUSE

OF

* UNDOING *

* **222** *

*Follow any
thread with
a*

*for a further
explanation,
tangent or
sometimes random
thread.*

* * * * *

236

*Because living well is not just about the house itself,
but the way you perform the inevitable duties we have sprinkled
eight lessons to live by throughout this book.*

* * *

When I asked my youngest
what she remembered from
when she was a baby, she
said, 'Our black floors'.
Floors really do matter.

FRANKLIN CUP
1977

FRANKLIN CUP 1979

*A*lthough it's considered unfashionable, I love the Impressionists. They were interested in capturing that moment before things change, knowing that the things we love the most are only with us for a very short time before they disappear. They celebrated the sort of happiness that only lasts a few minutes.

This is what styling is about for me. There is a skill to attending to these short-lived moments of satisfaction. Peaks of life are brief. Linen cupboards can crash from a ten to a two in no time. Addresses change. Happiness doesn't come in year-long blocks. Houses can be pawns and interior fulfilment can be fleeting or – if you are very, very lucky – forever.

It's Beautiful Here attempts to capture these moments of everyday paradise without making the mistake of thinking they will be permanent – but hoping hard that they might be.

Good interiors are all about myths. They are about hope. Turning bare walls into something that will pull at your heartstrings forever. It's possible to love your home. Your home can be the net that catches you and the ladder up which you climb.

Like all great myths, great houses are not necessarily about truth. They make the best out of difficult situations. They overwhelm any rational explanation. They comfort. They restore. They energise us and make the impossible possible. No-one can get through the snakes and ladders game of life without one, or the hope of one. This is the one thing we all share.

This book is a reflection on all that is about home. The world has too many interior pictures, but not enough stories. I wanted my house dreams to be delivered in a larger format than a bunch of tiny little squares, and I think you might too. Because it's only by going beneath the veneer of a house's proudest picture that we get to know a little bit more about ourselves.

How does a house belong in the *It's Beautiful Here* category if the barrier to entry is neither style nor money? For me, it's always been about how a house makes you feel, not its contents. A house in which the sum of its parts is more than its address or its shopping list.

This book is about those people who have by luck, chance or determination nailed that ever-elusive 'tone'. Please enjoy the motley crew of renters, Barbie Dreamhouse owners, tone-trained magicians and accidental interior heroes who are gathered here. Then, when you're done, know that this book is the perfect size to rest under your head while you lay on the floor looking up at the ceiling and consider the tone of your own home.

It's beautiful here . . .

PUNCH

DRUNK

Ali Satchell / Tina De Salis

Sydney

— ALI

  — HUSBAND

    — DAUGHTER no.1

      — DAUGHTER no.2

        — SON

          — DOG

'This home has had more work than Joan Rivers!' says Ali Satchell of her Federation style house that she has designed with her friend Tina de Salis, an interior designer and fellow colour appreciator.

'Ali knew that we had a big job ahead of us,' says Tina. 'It's structurally magnificent and well designed, but its proportions could have left it feeling cold.'

When large houses are renovated, it can seem as if the new has challenged the old to a duel. This transformation is all about the power play of that contrast. The house presents a quiet, demure front but when you venture inside it feels as if you have just headed off on a jetset holiday.

Ali's business, Sassafras Trading, imports treasures and wearables from all over the world, so this house really went to the right owner. When Ali sourced a three-metre chandelier in Bali, the house was designed around it. This grand gesture informed the staircase, which marks the point at which the original house gives way to the new build. At the front are traditional majestic living quarters but as you walk down the staircase the mood changes. Carpets are swapped for stone floors, Federation details are replaced by ethnic touches and the private rooms upstairs contrast with open spaces downstairs.

The key to making such huge statements and creating successful mood swings is to have a willing partner in crime, and Tina and Ali always intended to play their decorating cards within the realms of high contrast.

They started by amping things up in spaces that aren't defined by internal walls. 'We could counter the largeness of the space and create some internal, more intimate, moments that are little pockets of surprise using texture and tone,' says Tina. Large doors fold back to open up an outside room and pool. It's easy like a Sunday morning, with the subtle vibe of an Ibiza resort.

Knowing the gardens would be kept super lush and deep green, Tina doused the back of the house in a riot of her signature high-energy colour palette. Ali describes this back room as 'a little Stevie Nicks', but I think it's more Solange Knowles on summer break. 'The bright palette, tempered with the dark cabinetry and the view to the garden, works so well,' says Tina, who admits it took three years to get it right.

Like every good resort, there is a clever system of 'reveal and conceal'. A behind-the-scenes cupboard deals with the school gear, wardrobes are designed to always look neat, and a hidden, full-size laundry is serviced by a chute system. It takes a certain kind of person to keep a house like this looking perfect, and Ali admits her 'neat freak' tendencies have met their match here. 'I drive my family mad, but I operate best when it's set.'

But where do you go for family holidays when you have a house that is set up like a luxury resort? 'Cape du Couedic,'* says Ali. Think pristine beaches, a fur seal colony, kangaroo mobs and breathtaking landscapes where the only ornamentation is rock formations.

Lock yourself
in a loving duel
with a colour and
just stay there.

The people in your house
are much more important
than the house itself.

"

Who lives here?
Ali / ⓐ : Me, my husband David, and our three gorgeous children, Eliza (11), Olive (9) and Freddy (7).

If your house was a phrase, what would it be?
ⓐ : 'Home wasn't built in a day.' Jane Sherwood Ace (actor)

What is your most treasured possession?
ⓐ : A pair of Swedish vintage chairs covered in the most perfect Ralph Lauren leopard print – I'm a sucker for all things leopard!

What is your home's greatest extravagance?
ⓐ : Before we had kids and a mortgage, we did a trip to Darwin and Broome and bought an amazing Elizabeth Nyumi painting and works by Daniel Walbidi. These treasures hang in the entry of our home. It still makes us laugh that we bought them before we bought our first home. Also, the staircase and the fireplace jewellery! The handmade Moroccan copper screen is used cleverly as balustrades and a sliding fireplace screen. The repetition, scale and beauty of the ancient Islamic geometry adds a glamorous element that contrasts with the more earthy materials.

What is the most extravagant expense in the house?
ⓐ : The tree root mapping and engineering we needed to ensure that our beautiful Sydney gum could become a central feature of the extension. Without it, the outdoor area wouldn't have the continuity of warmth and soul that the rest of the house has.

What is the most over-rated real estate virtue?
ⓐ : Car parking. I'd rather have another room than a bedroom for my car.

Is your house covering up anything?
ⓐ : I was initially concerned at the endless Arts and Crafts mahogany but after extensive rectification, great design detail and lashings of white paint, she's sparkling new!

Where in your home are you the happiest?
ⓐ : The very rare peaceful moments that I catch in my husband's Eames chair, in the nook off our bedroom. The chair sits on the softest vintage Beni Ourain rug and is surrounded by a soothing dusty pink and lavender palette that is echoed in the two Leah Fraser paintings that watch over it.

What was your greatest renovation achievement?
ⓐ : Relocating the front door to create an oversized entry that gives the house a grand welcoming area.

What would you spend your last decorating dollar on?
ⓐ : A Joshua Yeldham painting.

Did you have a post-renovation realisation?
ⓐ : How underwhelming C-Bus is. [ⓜⓜ : For the uninitiated, C-Bus is a highly intelligent automation system that allows the home owner to draw curtains, turn the oven on or even lock themselves out entirely, without ever intending to.]

If your house was a singer, who would it be?
ⓐ : Stevie Nicks – eclectic, timeless, and a little bit boho.

Is there a colour you can't abide?
Tina / ⓣ : No, any opportunity for a colourfest!

What's your greatest domestic skill?
ⓐ : I'm an excellent bed maker and I arrange cushions like a boss.

What is the key to working with friends?
ⓣ : Designing beautiful homes that people love is largely about 'truth' and knowing who you are. If you can do this, it makes it easy. Ali has a very strong sense of who she is and what she likes. She was great at spearheading the direction and clear on what she loved and what she didn't.

Are two heads better than one?
ⓐ : Yes, if you're kindred spirits. You bounce off each other, which ultimately creates better ideas as well as ensuring your decisions are more considered. Tina and I have always done this – we have a mutual love of colour and a similar eye for the things we find beautiful. She definitely made me more adventurous than I would have been.

Is there a missed moment in the house?
ⓣ : A purpose-built outdoor area. The current one is large, open and certainly beautiful but I'd love it to actually feel like another living room.

ⓐ : An outside fireplace, please!

The house is a Pinterest dream, but what's it like to live in with three kids and a busy schedule?
ⓐ : Fantastic! There's loads of space to get away from each other and hide, yet several zones where we can all be together comfortably. It also works beautifully. Tina and I spent many hours in the early part of the project considering functionality. We considered everything from how I cook in the kitchen to where I wrap the birthday presents, so that things were put in the right position and there was adequate storage. The entire southern side of the house was allocated to 'services', including a butler's pantry, locker room, small office and laundry. The locker room has purpose-built cupboards for all of us, as well as things like our bags and sports equipment. All that can be unpacked and stored out of sight, right next to the laundry.

❋

KATIE MARX & GREG HATTON

HOW TO BALANCE HOME AND WORK

Katie Marx is a florist whose reputation has been built on generous foraged dream scenes, helped along by her fairytale house/workshop* in an old butter factory called Butterland. The patchwork of original wooden block floors and enamel tiles in the old factory's cavernous space carry the spirit of hard work and beauty for her and her partner, Greg Hatton, a furniture maker and landscaper. With two small daughters and three creative businesses, here are Katie's tips on how they manage to balance it all.

1

First, succumb to the fact that things take time. Good things cannot be rushed. Social media presents life in a super-fast way but anything worth doing is always slowly baked. Especially when there are small children around!

2

If you work from home, divide your time not your home. I find it impossible to have a 'work' space and a 'home' space. It serves us better all as one. Your own discipline around what you do and how you switch between rest and work is the key to a successful home business, rather than creating a physical division.

3

Don't attempt anything important until you have the children sorted and dealt with! Your head, hands and heart do need to be connected and it's virtually impossible to do this if it's going crazy behind the scenes.

4

Don't be hard on yourself and always stay true to your ideals. Working for yourself is an honourable thing at the best of times, and doing it alongside your partner and family is worthy of applause! Even if it's not forever, it's a time you will definitely look back on and proudly say, 'We did it!'

IS

NOT

A

DOCTOR

Phil Van Huynh

Melbourne

Despite his extensive book collection, Phil Van Huynh is not one of the six million readers of Marie Kondo's *The Life-Changing Magic of Tidying Up*. While Marie and Phil are at opposite ends of the spectrum (they could probably feature in a worldwide televised debate!) there are some genuine commonalities to their approaches. At first glance, Marie could come across as a classic fun-spoiling OCD sufferer from Tokyo. By comparison, Phil could come across as a maniac from Melbourne who buys whatever he wants, whenever he wants. No matter which way you swing, we all know Kondo's proven joy-sparking methods are about order and beauty. And at the core of it, so are Phil's.

After securing his double-storey warehouse three years ago with the intention of just renovating the amenities, Phil decided to put his time and investment into its contents instead. The result is a heady experience for the unsuspecting guest. Winding down a back street, dodging brothels and over-branded cafes (this combination is solid proof that you have bought in an up-and-coming area!), you approach a roller door with an 'I am right, you are wrong' sign on the buzzer. Upstairs – past a warren of rooms and workshops that are used for installation floral work – a free-form nirvana awaits. As far as real estate square metres go, there are lots, but there is no chance you'd ever find misplaced keys in this labyrinth of cut foliage, plants, sundries and contents.

And for the record Phil is not a doctor. But he is overly qualified in his love for plants, flowers and things.

*In a time where minimalist same-same houses speak of
'curation grading' and 'negative space journeys',
let's take a look at five areas where Phil has
unknowingly taken Marie Kondo's advice.*

1

⟨ *Phil Tackles Categories, Not Rooms* ⟩

He buys up big on ceramics. Then books. Then bandanas. Then scissors.
Then limited-edition pyjamas. Then incense accessories. Then he scatters all
these things in every room. This is what makes it a treasure-trove experience,
rather than a crazy-uncle-gone-mad one.

2

⟨ *Phil Respects His Belongings* ⟩

Kondo suggests we should consider our clothing's feelings. Phil seems to
know that the Astier de Villatte and Alana Wilson ceramics should probably live
on different surfaces, and that the almost-impossible-to-get hunter green Staub
kettle won't be happy in a corner spot, but requires a central position that shows
off its flattering profile.

3

⟨ *Phil Knows Nostalgia is Not His Friend* ⟩

There are three things he truly cares about: a photograph of his mother
taken before they arrived in Australia as immigrants, his grandfather's pen and
a letter from someone dear to him. Everything else is a temporary high.

4

⟨ *Phil Knows to Fold, Not Hang* ⟩

There is no other way to handle 200 coloured polo shirts or 100 bandanas.
His housekeeping looks chaotic at first glance, but it's actually Marie-worthy
methodical and verging on Virgo.

5

⟨ *Phil Only Collects Things He Really Loves* ⟩

He goes for thrilling purchases that spark joy. 'It's the hard thing about
choosing to live away,' he says, 'but it is just all stuff and plants'.

A good house is like
when someone hugs
you back harder.
Come to mumma.

GOD
SAVE
THE
KING
LE MEILLEUR LAIT
MARSEILLE
LE MEILLEUR LAIT
MARSEILLE
LE MEILLEUR LAIT
MARSEILLE
LE MEILLEUR LAIT
Rad. Althaeae
Eibischwurzel
Fol. Salviae
Salbeiblätter
Sem. Lini
Leinsamen

Who lives here?
Basically my plants.

Where are you answering these questions from?
I started at work in the studio at Emily Thompson Flowers in New York. We were in the middle of a spring heatwave. This Q+A has travelled home to Melbourne, then to Paris and London, and I'm finally finishing it off back in New York at home with Bruce Springsteen's 'Secret Garden' on repeat. I've been revisiting his classics since seeing him in concert in Paris recently.

Has Springsteen informed your answers?
I wish! I'm not the strongest with words but you wouldn't accept my answers in floral form!

What is your idea of perfect home happiness?
Friends gathered around the table eating a home-cooked meal by candlelight.

What is your house's greatest fear?
Closed-minded people.

Which living person do you most admire?
Australian florist and entrepreneur Joost Bakker.

What is your home's greatest extravagance?
An Anna-Wili Highfield paper sculpture of a wolf.

What is the most over-rated real estate virtue?
Self-cleaning ovens.

What do people say when they come to your house?
'Why is there a giant inflatable duck in your living room?'

Where in your house are you the happiest?
Downstairs, tinkering in the studio and photographing flowers.

What is your house's greatest achievement?
The number of people it can sleep.

What is your parallel universe house or place?
A farm in the Cotswolds.

What is the most extravagant expense in the house?
Industrial battery acid vases from Tarlo and Graham.

What would you spend your last decorating dollar on?
Anything by London-based furniture designer Faye Toogood.

What do you find beautiful?
Human compassion.

What's on your bedside table?
Wherever I am, I always have a posy of foraged flowers.

What was your childhood like?
All the best days were spent with my Grandpa in the vegetable garden.

What is your greatest domestic skill?
Making fresh pasta from scratch and hanging a picture straight.

What's one thing you wish everybody knew about?
Yves Klein blue and The Laundress Signature Detergent.

When you are away, do you pine for home?
Always, home is where my plants and my heart are.

Is home where the heart is, or where the hat is?
Both. I collect hats from my travels and they make their way back home with me.

What is your proudest flower moment?
Working on Miso's *Silent Landscape* exhibition. It was an inverted landscape of land and sky that was suspended above people's heads as they viewed her artworks. I worked on it from midnight until the crack of dawn, at which point I went home, showered, and started work on a flower run.

What are best plants to leave neglected?
Succulents.

What is your favourite flower variety?
Australian native flowers.

How do you manage to have so much stuff yet it doesn't look like a red hot mess?
Bringing in so many plants for greenery is my way of replicating the landscape where I am happiest – outside. Less is more, but more can be great as well. A high ceiling helps too! And my maximalist nature wants more. There is order and method to it, with some OCD thrown in.

What can't money buy?
The satisfaction of fulfilling your dreams.

✳

CHRISTINA McLEAN

HOW TO DECK YOUR HALLS BOHO

Textile designer Christina McLean is seriously at her happiest when she's trawling through flea markets, bazaars and bric-a-brac stores for fibre art. For those of you who fall hard for textiles, here are her tips on how to best show your wares around the home.

LOOK (AND HANG) IN UNEXPECTED PLACES

When confronted by somewhere like Les Puces (the Paris flea market), make a point of looking in at least one shop you would NEVER usually set foot in. When in the not-you shop, turn the place upside down. I swear your treasure will be there. Then consider placing the treasure in an unusual spot when you're back home. One of my most-loved pieces is a Kuba embroidered raffia cloth. I have it on my wall in my dining room and whenever I have people over for dinner it's a talking point.

⬦⬦⬦⬦⬦⬦

LOOK TWICE AT THE TIMEWORN

Threadbare pieces are less valued in textile-rich cultures, but I believe them to be the perfect tonic for western walls. The imperfections and wear are interesting and you can usually haggle harder, given their condition. In 1996 I was in Jaisalmer, Rajasthan, and I was besotted with the Banjara textiles of the region. One stallholder was trying to sway me against purchasing a really big, old wedding canopy. It was an appliquéd piece from Gujarat – faded, worn and threadbare – but I adored it and I wasn't leaving without it. It now has pride of place on my bedroom wall. I stare at it when I'm lying in bed.

CITY STREETS

Sometimes you just can't manage extra travel time. If you can't get out of the city, you have to accept that you will pay a higher price for treasures, no matter what continent you are travelling and trawling in. If you are in Delhi, I suggest Janpath Market (a street market) and Chandni Chowk (an alleyway full of textiles and haberdashery).

⬦⬦⬦⬦⬦⬦

MIX IT UP

Hang carpets on the wall. Suspend ropes to display your lobster pots. Make beautiful pairings by putting kimonos or tunics next to paintings or ceramic wall pieces. Handwoven garments often make perfect throws over your lounge or can be hung at the top of your curtain as a textile pelmet. Vintage Rabari dowry bags look fantastic on the backs of chairs.

⬦⬦⬦⬦⬦⬦

THE BEAUTIFUL AND THE VULNERABLE

When you are investing in textile treasures, remember that the more fragile the piece, the more susceptible to insects it will be. Jute, linen and cotton work with more fibre strength are more easily found and more affordable, and can work wonderfully over a metal rod or a curtain rail for a quick, easy and cost-effective display. Fine silks should be framed behind glass – a costly expense.

BLIND

FAITH

Anna Charlesworth

Sydney

Did you know that Elsie de Wolfe reinvented the bathroom? But what do Elsie, America's first interior designer who made her name during the peak of pomp, and Anna Charlesworth, an unpretentious glass and metal artist, have in common?

Elsie de Wolfe took her inspiration from the 18th-century *toilette* ritual where women received admiring callers in their dressing-room boudoirs (google William Hogarth's *Marriage à-la-mode* paintings for glorious proof, go on). She reinstated her bathroom as a glamorous entertaining space complete with zebra banquette, a fully loaded bar cart and a bath mat that did double duty as a yoga mat. (I stuck up a picture of Elsie in Plow Pose* while I was renovating my bathroom, as a reminder that they can have a sense of occasion if we let them.) Similarly, not discounting her set of covetable Cassina Cab chairs and Knoll three-seater, the toilet is the best seat in Anna's beautiful house. (It's a Starck for Duravit.)

Anna commissioned her friends, arbiters of interior taste Don McQualter and Julie Meacham, to design the house that she shares with her husband, their daughter and their dog, Donna. 'We knew that Don and Julie had better taste than us, so it was easy to defer to their ideas,' she says.

Bathrooms are usually designed with a heavy hand, almost like mini-me kitchens, but Don's masterstroke of a bathroom for Anna is as light as air with a top note of patchouli. It is ridiculously beautiful. Don was inspired by Indian railway rest rooms – oversized and sparse. For two people, it's out on a limb in terms of size – another designer could easily have made it another bedroom. Don thought the colour on the wall should be part Frank Sinatra, part bad make-up. Anna says, 'I had an appalling French teacher at school in the 70s who wore a similar shade of foundation that finished at her chin line. But, in the context of the space, it's a colour I don't get sick of.'

When it comes to maintaining the bathroom mood, Anna suggests avoiding direct overhead lighting. 'I've got recessed lighting and small cameo lights I made for the wall to ensure it felt welcoming.' It is so successful that people find it hard to leave. 'People do seem to stay in there for a long time!' says Anna, who designed doorhandles and other brass touchpoints in the house, as well as all the lighting.

This home plays the juxtaposition card without coming across all slap-in-the-face-super-high-impact. Instead, it features simmering combinations like gloss peach paint paired with chalky Elba stone, terrazzo floors bookended with tallowwood ceilings and a double Aga facing imposing full-length glass doors. 'I love its ability to expand for family celebrations, but then contract back to a cosy house for the three of us.'

Any advice for others working on their own projects with friends? 'Be open-minded. There can be no hard and fast design rules with any renovation, as a lot can change over the time of the build,' says Anna. 'We are so lucky. Don and Julie gave us a house we love. I sometimes feel like I'm an impostor here!'

And for those that want to channel the Charlesworth's throne, just add noble proportions, engage friends who have flawless taste and go forth, do a de Wolfe, and manipulate space like a boss!

Blue is bliss.
Get intimate with it.
Your life will be
better for it.

What is your idea of perfect home happiness?
Three humans and a dog, and a roof that doesn't leak.

What is your house's greatest fear?
That it's the ugliest* in the land.

Which living person do you most admire?
Our daughter, Nina.

What is your greatest extravagance?
Travel.

What is your home's greatest extravagance?
Access to natural light.

What is the most over-rated real estate virtue?
Ensuites.

If your house was a phrase, what would it be?
Mi casa es tu casa.

Where in your home are you the happiest?
Wherever the sun is shining.

*If you could change one thing about the house,
what would it be?*
Nothing to see here! Next question . . .

What is your house's greatest achievement?
Its cheerfulness.

What is your parallel universe house or place?
One of those fantastic houses in Brazil where
the jungle is growing through the dwelling areas.

When is your home at its lowest depth of misery?
When it's unoccupied.

What is your home's greatest extravagance?
The heated hiperfloor.

What would you spend your last decorating dollar on?
Bed linen.

What do you find beautiful?
Light and greenery.

What's on your bedside table?
Half-read books, headphones and little images
of landscapes by Lisa Walker.

What's the worst thing your house has ever done?
It locked me out.

If your house was a singer, who would it be?
Judith Durham.

Where will you grow old, and what does it look like?
This house, with a ramp for the two steps,
but transported to the south of France.

What was your childhood like?
Hectic with big bouts of boredom –
I'm one of seven children.

Is your way of life now a response to your formative years?
It can't be any other way.

What's your greatest domestic skill?
Eating.

Is your home a summer house or a winter house?
Both.

What's one design idea you wish everyone knew?
Get the proportions right and everything else will follow.

Are you decoratively optimistic?
Always. Things can always be changed.
It's not life or death.

*How does your creative work life meld with your
family life?*
My work life rarely crosses over into my family life.
I'm lucky in some ways that my work is a forty-minute
drive from home. When I'm at work I can't be
distracted . . . in theory.

What are the potential dangers of working with friends?
I don't envy anyone trying to design or build a dream
dwelling for someone else. It's a fraught idea from
the outset.

*Does an interior designer need to know you well to
deliver the house of your dreams?*
They need to keep the conversation open but not
bombard you with choices.

*Do you feel compelled to be a super-good cook now that you
have a super-good kitchen?*
Pete has always been a super-good cook. The kitchen is his
favourite place to be. It is a pleasure to cook with a great
stove. I remember cooking scones for the builders when
we first moved in. I thought I was a legend.

*It's obvious you believe in the manifesto 'buy once, buy
better'. What's been your best design investment so far?*
Our Knoll sofa. It's going in for its third reupholstering.
It just keeps on going.

PERCENTAGE OF BLACK

Camille Walala

London

The name Camille means 'free born' and Walala translates loosely to 'ooh la la'. Walala is the name an ex-boyfriend made up for Camille and it stuck. She was raised in a village in Provence, France, with a population of 300 but her papa insisted his beloved daughter move to London to learn English. Luckily for the world she followed her father's wishes, but turned her back on her original degree in French literature and studied textile design at the University of Brighton instead.

Artists Victor Vasarely and Bridget Riley and the South African Ndebele tribe are major influences for her, but the real drivers of her clashing and combining style are her parents. Her architect father's minimal apartment in Paris is devoted to straight lines and her mother's house in Provence is a magnet for anything Mediterranean in palette and African in textiles.

Camille has given the world small bites of her brilliance through clothing ranges and nail sticker collaborations. On a larger scale, nightclubs, brutalist buildings, and even Facebook's head office have been infectiously 'ooh la la'ed. She proves that it's not where you take things from but where you take them to that counts.

What's happening in Copenhagen now is also what's happening in Collingwood and Chicago, so travel is a big part of her work life. It's also how she recharges from the physical aspect of the installations. 'Mini-breaks are my circuit breakers, I like to try and get as many as I can.'

Her East London home might be small but it is mighty and showcases both sides of her decorating lineage. Camille is ridiculously domesticated – a total bon vivant when it comes to music and food – and her apartment is a glorious testimony to making the most of a rental tenancy. Super savvy with her decorating energy, it took Camille and a friend just one weekend to make over the apartment after she removed the carpet and got her neighbour onto the paint job. She has made feature walls out of tape, created rooms within rooms and often cooks for a dozen people from her maisionette kitchen. Her happiest times are when she is dancing in her lounge room.

I am dreaming of the day when we can stream universal good vibes through Radio Ooh La La and see a Walala aeroplane flying through the skies to its destination of Happy Place. I get the feeling that she is just warming up, don't you? The best is yet to come. Because what she is all about is what the world needs a dose of now – more 'ooh la las', more vibrant communities, more jolts of joy and more spaces that lift the spirit. And definitely more lounge room dancing!

Stripes are magical –
just ask any beach
umbrella in the
south of France.

ROY LICHTENSTEIN IN HIS STUDIO

VICTOR VASARELY

ADVENTURES OF THE BLACK SQUARE
Abstract Art and Society 1915–2015

PRESTEL

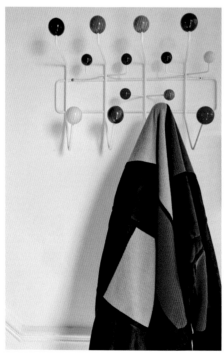

Find one bit
of wonderment
in your house.
Even if you
have to put it
there yourself.

Who lives here?
Me and Pecorino the cat.

Are you a gypsy by birth or choice?
Choice!

Which living person do you admire most?
Grayson Perry.

What is your idea of perfect home happiness?
A house full of people, with a big wooden table
outside for long lunches.

What is your house's greatest fear?
Smelling damp.

What is your greatest extravagance?
A pair of Vivienne Westwood shoes.

What is your home's greatest extravagance?
I have been very reasonable so far.

Is your house missing anything?
Yes, I wish it had a fireplace.

Who are you influenced by?
Bauhaus, Ndbele and the artist Sonia Delaunay.

What do you find beautiful?
I went on holiday to Spain and discovered
La Muralla Roja, a housing project in Alicante
that was designed by the architect Ricardo Bofill.

What's on your bedside table?
Lavender oil, of course!

What was your childhood like?
I grew up in Provence in the south of France
in a very colourful house, climbing cherry trees
and playing with my rabbit Kikinou.

Tell us about your family's summer house in France.
It has been for years a house full of family and friends,
where everyone cooks or brings something for the
table…we spend hours eating! I love having a siesta
after lunch on the sofa or in the hammock in the
garden, before going in the pool later.

What is your most treasured possession?
An African beaded, bright, bold and graphic basket
from the Ivory Coast that my grandma brought back
from her trip there in the 60s.

What do you value most about your work?
When it makes people smile.

What does downtime look like for you?
Going to restaurants, spending time with friends
and mini-breaks.

*Do you treat a residential installation the same
as a public building?*
I am always trying to feel the place first. I look at the
surroundings and the colours, as I don't want them to
clash with the house and my designs. But I make sure
I create a harmony.

Are you a packaging snob?
Yes, the less packaging the better!

*Why haven't you been asked to paint
the Sydney Opera House?*
I wouldn't dare touch this beauty…but if I could
do a projection for Vivid Sydney one day that would
be so amazing!

ENOUGH

ALREADY

Emma Abrahams

Melbourne

Jeweller Emma Abrahams steals time. She answers my questions in the car while her son is at Scouts. When her muse Jean Paul Gaultier was in town, she worked all-nighters for two weeks to present him with a 65-piece striped sapphire skull ring.

People see her work and drop a deposit. She loves couture and would commission clothes regularly if she could. She has a six-burner Viking stove with a griddle plate that she uses every night. She runs her family like a boss and demands quality time with her serial entrepreneur husband, Justin. She has perspex boxes made for her shoes, but often wears the cowboy boots she bought in Texas when she was sixteen. Her jewellery business, Heart of Bone, might be new, but she has been making beautiful red-hot messes forever.

The story of her beautiful house starts fifteen years ago, when she specialised in 18th- and 19th-century paint and gilding work. Justin was a client, but it was all of four seconds before they fell in love and moved in together. Many houses, businesses and projects later, the family home they share with their two children is a slick, single-level compound – 70s in spirit, but a melting pot in terms of its fill.

This house is the result of two people whose individual tastes do not overlap, but who made joint decisions on a few key wicked additions sourced just for this house. 'I chase luxury, opulence and humour,' says Emma, 'and Justin steers more towards balance, simplicity and design. But we always seem to find that meeting point in a genuine way.'

The spectacular starts with a classic 70s oversized entry door, then continues through some pretty serious rooms that are set with all the right pieces from all the right people. Past the sunken sitting room and the formal dining room is a generous kitchen that marks the start of the informal spaces.

Disparity is the key to the house's overall drama. Masculine materials with sensitive flourishes. Iranian textiles with Italian collectables. Turkish stone with a locally made 'Ride Me' neon sign.* Ethnography merges with Memphis.

Decisiveness is their combined advantage. 'We have an idea then we go straight for it. It's the same at work, I prefer to skip extensive drawings and go straight into the wax carving. I feel very lucky to have these skills but sometimes it feels like a curse too. It's an overwhelming desire that can come before domestic needs and that can be hard to manage.' Her swift resolve gets results. Like the night she created a picture of the house using images of the 70s wallpaper from the original house and an Arkleyesque airbrush tool, then had it printed and hung on the kitchen wall by the week's end.

Emma is a glorious trifecta of sophistication, action and spontaneity and everyone in her orbit gets to share in it. 'My idea of happiness is to cook all day, call my friends and family over to a table full of food, and have everyone running around dancing. Basically this house is one giant party house masquerading as a family home.'

Making two worlds
collide will always
look progressive.

What is your house's greatest fear?
Winter. It's a long story – we got the heating
a bit wrong but basically we are walking around
at night in puffer jackets.

What piece has the most of you in it?
Probably our dining table. It's a reproduction of
a 15th-century English table that seats eighteen.
I hand-polished it and carved our initials in it and
it has an iron dog chain attached to the bottom.

What is your greatest extravagance?
Clothing. I love the process, the creativity and
collaboration, the individuality and luxurious nature
of it. Playing dress-ups is my most loved creative and
inspiring pastime. Taking on different characters
and being whoever I choose is a form of creative
expression for me.

What is your home's greatest extravagance?
The stone. It's called Alba and it's Turkish. We managed
to get a lovely bright white Alba with subtle hues of
grey and lavender. It arrived in a twenty-foot container.
Nowadays the same quarry produces a much murkier
grey stone. Ours has such beautiful qualities. It climbs
up from the floor, up the walls in the bathrooms and
powder room to ceiling height. It's both masculine
and soft at the same time.

What is your most treasured possession?
We kept the bottle from the Cristal we drank on the
night we got engaged. It's in a glass dome along with
a rock from the beach where Justin wrote 'EMMA
WILL YOU MARRY ME' in giant letters. We went
back to the beach after we drank the champagne and
the tide had come in and washed it away. As if it never
happened. I'm so glad we took one of those rocks. Not
just as souvenirs but as a reminder that everything can
change in the blink of an eye and you have to enjoy
every moment. I'm not really a nostalgic person nor
a romantic but in this time, this house, this space,
these are treasured.

What is the house's lowest depth of misery?
I really deeply feel that the house is lonely when we
go away. We come back and it's cold and standoffish.
It smells a bit dry and seems to radiate a 'where have
you been?' attitude. It always takes a while to settle
in and get all cosy again.

What is your family's most-used possession?
My husband's grandma's 18th-century Venetian chaise
longue. Both kids fight about who gets to sit on it when
they're watching TV.

What is your favourite possession?
I did a contra deal on a pair of 19th-century Florentine
parlour chairs when I was working as an antique
restorer. I was completely broke but I had to have them.

What is the most extravagant expense in the house?
The cool room. Worth every cent.

What would you spend your last decorating dollar on?
Chairs. I'm obsessed with 18th-century French chairs.

Is your house male or female?
Female.

What's your greatest domestic skill?
I can cook. I used to work in restaurants as
a cook while I was at uni. I learnt a few tricks.

What's one thing you wish everyone knew?
People ask me all the time how I can live in such
a white, minimalist space, given my artistic
temperament and eclectic taste. The answer is that
I'm naturally very messy and I adore clutter, but this
house helps me clean my mind. It calms me.

*How do you merge your instincts with those of your
highly informed and intelligent husband?*
We complement each other in an easy and fun way.
We have respect and admiration for each other's design
tendencies and leanings. It's always a joy, not a chore.
We never seem to disagree on that stuff.

*Heart of Bone is both soft and hard, beautiful
and sinister – is your work a metaphor for your
own mind, body and soul?*
You got me!

Is your studio a salvation or an obligation?
It's both. It depends how busy it gets but,
either way, I'd be lost without a space to truly
let go and express myself unhindered.

THREE

DOORED

HOUSE

Camie Lyons

Sydney

If you believe in domestic destiny, you will love Camie Lyons's story. And even if you don't believe in a higher real estate power, you will enjoy her ramshackle decadent house tale all the same.

The epic sculptor returned to Sydney ten years ago with a Belgian husband, their two young sons and a rich CV of international public works. Camie was actively manifesting a corner block with a garden, enough room for her family and a studio. Additional mandatories were a separate shed where she and her blowtorch could go at it for hours on end. Plus, it had to be near the action of Sydney, and affordable.

'Being a sculptor, not a merchant banker, meant I could see the right foundations but couldn't necessarily afford them!' Camie remembers.

Come auction day, a humble bid landed the corner cottage they now call home in her lap. The rest is home–life history.

'Never moving,' she says of her Victorian spread in Petersham, in Sydney's inner west.

As her boys play down the family end of the house, she downs tools in the studio and follows through on an urge to melt some metal while her paintwork dries.

Camie's dinner parties are notorious. They happen around her grandmother's bequeathed table, which up until now 'never made any sense to me and was always a bit of a bulky burden'. The dining room is at the other end of the house from the kitchen, which Camie says brings a 'sense of occasion to every meal'. The ritual of carting kit down to the table, setting it up and enjoying the open studio next door – and often a roaring fire as well – is her daily reward for the long hours she puts in at the studio while juggling family life.

How does she manage two roles under one roof? By spreading them out in the same space. A left turn down the dilapidated hallway takes you to Camie's studio, where her drawings, paintings and sculptures are created. A right turn gets you to the bedrooms, shared living spaces and kitchen, which take real advantage of the L-shaped corner block.

Movement is the common theme that runs through this ex-dancer's work. But it is also what runs this busy house. The flow of family life is intertwined with the demands of her successful art practice.

'Life imitating art and art imitating life,' she says. 'What is also great is having my seven-year-old being able to weld with me in the garage. Todra's friends come over and literally can't believe their eyes when we melt bronze.'*

'Once, when Todra was about four, we walked past a very noisy and industrious worksite, the shocking sound of grinders assaulting the street. Todra turned to me, smiled sweetly and said, "Ohhhhhh, some poor mummy is working".' As luck would have it, her charming neighbour on the workshop side is stone deaf. 'And he makes the most amazing pastizzi.'

Some houses want you to do good work. Some houses are enablers. Camie has found her nirvana in this house. 'Despite the usual artistic barriers, I feel like this house is always encouraging, keeping me buoyant and focused on my end goals.'

The ability to
experience beauty
is one of the best
reasons for living.

Owner–occupier:
many people own
houses but few really
'occupy' them.

"

What is your idea of perfect home happiness?
Laughter, good food, cosying up in front of an open fire and enjoying yet another high-action movie with my sons, Todra and Oskar, and my husband, Sverker.

What is your house's greatest fear?
Being too perfect! It just wouldn't suit her, she spent years collecting those colours in the hallway and shifting about to get those cracks just right – if she gets a total facelift she will become one of those generic Hollywood starlets who are left with no expression.

Which living person do you most admire?
Right now I am totally enamoured with Ann Thomson. I went to her tribute at the National Art School just last week – AMAZING. She is eighty-three and still producing the most vibrant, relevant and exciting work. She looks amazing – ramrod straight and long back, dressed in a very groovy black number with lashings of red lipstick – she is everything I hope to be. She is just such beautiful evidence of passion keeping you hugely energetic and generous and contributing to life's dialogue. I admire her and those like her greatly. It's humbling, and it reminds me just how much I have to learn.

If your house was a phrase what would it be?
Grande Olde Dame.

What is the best spot in the house?
I love curling up in my dad's old armchair in the studio. I miss him and it reminds me of him.

What is your house's greatest achievement?
Keeping her dignity.

What is your parallel universe house or place?
Sverker's father has an incredibly special place in the Swedish forest. There are not enough words to describe how 'other' and divine the land is. It's all soft and silent and hums in the incredibly whimsical twilight. We have spent a lot of time there over the years. That's our magic place.

What is the most extravagant expense in the house?
Sverker just bought me what was advertised on eBay as 'the most beautiful window in the world'. It does come close and we can't wait to put it in. It's the beginning of our bathroom renovation.

What would you spend your last decorating dollar on?
A huge French mirror for the entrance – it's on my list.

What do you find beautiful?
Quirks.

What's the worst thing your house has ever done?
About a week after finishing my studio, which took months of painstaking restoration, we were rudely awoken during the night by a huge 'whip' sound. It was the wall cracking wide open again. It brought tears to our eyes. We just leave it now – it insists on being there.

Where will you grow old, and what does it look like?
It could very possibly be this house – but I doubt it, we travel too much. It could be in Sweden, I'd like that. Also – I'm not going out quietly, I'm powering on until the very end, just like Ann Thomson. I'll be tripping over sculptures and champagne glasses, I'll have as many pets as I like and I will be cantankerous and opinionated. I'll love my people fiercely and totally spoil the grandchildren. There will be mysterious things in pots in the kitchen and flowers everywhere. And I'll be out in the back shed, welding.

What was your childhood like?
I grew up in a country town, one of six children, loads of unsupervised time – I just really floated about in my own universe. I think that is another reason I was drawn to this house; I wanted the boys to have more space and a garden to get lost in.

Is your home a summer house or a winter house?
It's an even split.

Do you love or hate Pinterest? Colour coding books? Butcher tiles?
Hate is too strong a word, but I dislike all of those things a lot.

Are you generally decoratively optimistic?
I'm decoratively flexible.

✳

REBECCA WIGGINS

HOW TO LIVE
WITH SMALL PEOPLE

Rebecca and her husband are teachers who live with their lively sons
in a renovated cottage in glorious Tasmania. There is no-one better than
Mrs Wiggins to offer some sage advice about how to live with small people.

EMBRACE THE CHAOS
AS MUCH AS YOU CAN

Invest in beautiful open-ended toys that have
aesthetic value. I found this difficult initially,
as I was so particular about where things went, but
after some time I decided to embrace the still-life
Lego creations and the wooden block towers and
put them in prominent places around the home.

∞∞∞∞∞∞

ADD GREENERY

Put plants in all the rooms, especially bedrooms.
A beautiful fern sitting atop a vintage desk in my
littlest's bedroom, next to his toadstool lamp, is so
endearing that I enjoy being in his space.

∞∞∞∞∞∞

PICTURE BOOKS ARE PRICELESS

Displayed in bedrooms in old suitcases, crates,
and baskets or as a miniature library, picture books
bring so much warmth to a home. Gather classics
from your childhood home as well as new picture
books with perfect covers. You can and should
judge a book by its cover!

∞∞∞∞∞∞

WHEN CHOOSING FURNITURE
FOR LITTLE PEOPLE, GO VINTAGE,
SECONDHAND OR BESPOKE

So much more character is brought into
a room when a piece is one of a kind.

∞∞∞∞∞∞

YOUR CHILDREN'S ART SHOULD
BECOME PART OF YOUR ART COLLECTION

Frame a few choice pieces and add them to your
French hang or simply lean them against the wall.

DON'T BE AFRAID TO PUT
BEAUTIFUL ART IN CHILDREN'S ROOMS

We have bold vintage posters in the boys'
bedrooms. One beautiful piece speaks more
than numerous fashionable prints. Showing them
you appreciate art will assist in their development
and appreciation for beauty.

∞∞∞∞∞∞

WHEN YOU TRAVEL,
COLLECT PIECES THAT SPEAK TO YOU

We often buy a wooden toy or a key ring. On our
next adventure, I hope to collect stickers to cover
our luggage. Postcards are another sweet collection
for children to choose at new destinations. Create a
pin board, inside a cupboard or wall, and document
your family adventures, be it to the national park
an hour from your home, or somewhere on the
other side of the world.

∞∞∞∞∞∞

TREASURE YOUR FAMILY MEMORIES

We have some very loved FLATOUT bears,
which we gave our children on the day they were
born. Soon they won't want to sleep with them
anymore, and when that day arrives they are off
to the framer. I will hang them with love in
our master bedroom. Swoon.

∞∞∞∞∞∞

MAKE YOUR HOUSE THE ONE
EVERYONE WANTS TO BE AT!

I am hoping that, as the years pass, our home
is where the children and their friends will want
to be – by the pool in summer, eating icy poles
and a sausage from the barbecue!

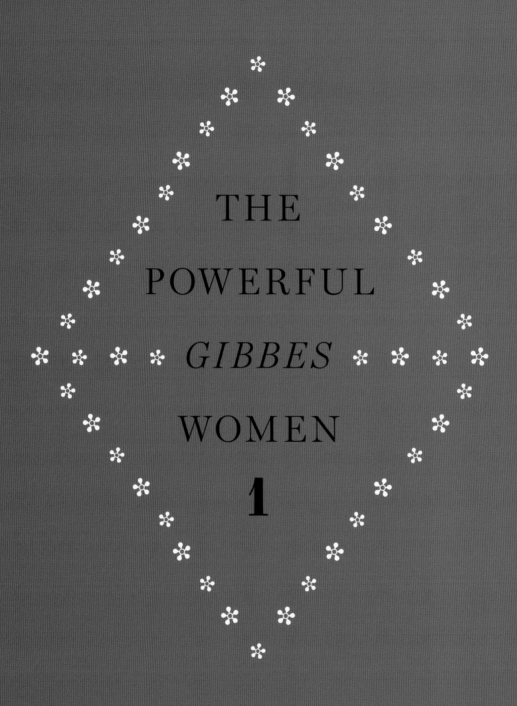

THE
POWERFUL
GIBBES
WOMEN
1

Caroline Gibbes

Melbourne

  — HUSBAND

    — DAUGHTER No.1

      — DAUGHTER No.2

        — DOG

She is something else. She just is. It's too easy to put her in the *Mad Men* category. Sure she's stylish, has sashay and can make a mean martini, but Caroline is not a cliché – she's an original. Her joie de vivre cannot be adequately represented by a hashtag or an adjective.

Caroline and husband Drew live life at what I can only describe as a higher level. Genuine enthusiasts for life, they meet at the bar for a well-earned 'congratulations, you made it' drink at the end of every day. They host dinner parties and barbecues and are the doting parents of twin girls who have hectic sporting and school schedules. Working during school hours enables Caroline to keep the business moving without it overtaking their family life completely. She works from home, in a converted garage downstairs. Her work week is ritualised by the auction houses where she inevitably buys something for a client and something for her and Drew. 'The house has an endless capacity and I doubt it will ever be filled,' says Caroline.

There is no eye rolling from Drew, only sheer encouragement. 'She has truly exceptional taste,' he says.

'In fact, we have similar tastes, so he's happily to let me rip,' she adds.

Their modernist masterpiece makes for fluid family living, but what is it like to cook in an original 60s kitchen? 'Look, I am not mad about cooking, but it has to be done and the layout is fantastic. The original appliances are still going strong and, if I am honest, the orange tiles give you pep to get on with the job.'

Where does it come from, her innate sense of interior swag? There are hints of Hollywood film designer Tony Duquette and top notes of the irreverent Ricky Clifton along with traces of distinct flair from her gorgeous mother (meet Virginia Gibbes on page 96), but it is mostly from a lifetime of experiences. 'Memories of all the incredible things I've seen in my life have stuck, festered, and come out the other end in all the odd things I do,' she says. It's also how she has managed to resurrect the taboo Australian 70s with great aplomb, splicing it up with a mélange of materials, textural collisions, exquisite cabinetry and unique finds.

When asked about the provenance of their amazing fibre art bedhead in the master room, Caroline replies, 'Oh that thing. It is actually a fabulous shag rug I found. Drew just made a metal frame for it, and voila!'

Yes, totally voila!

Your idea of perfect home happiness?
Sitting at the kitchen table surrounded
by craft crap and my girls.*

If your house was a singer, who would it be?
Shirley Bassey.

What's your greatest domestic skill?
Over decorating.

What is your house's greatest fear?
War and persecution. It was built by survivors of the
Holocaust and the high quality of the build means
a cyclone wouldn't budge it and no-one can get in
unless they're invited.

What did they get right in the 60s?
Everything. Generosity of space, great flow,
lots of light and full-on decorating.

*I knew you when you lived in a Victorian terrace,
but this house seems to be your perfect match.
Are you still looking for other amazing trophy houses?*
Drew keeps his eyes peeled, so we do snoop around
quite a bit.

Which living person do you most admire?
My mother. She's always content.

What is your greatest extravagance?
Absentee bidding at auction houses.

What is your home's greatest extravagance?
All the woodwork is bespoke and was crafted
by Dario Zoureff.

What is the most over-rated real estate virtue?
Boring big white rooms.

Is your house covering up anything?
Didn't you notice there are two layers of wallpaper?!

What quality do you like most in a room?
An interesting floor-to-ceiling treatment –
it's not used enough, in my opinion.

If your house was a phrase, what would it be?
A modernist masterpiece for fluid family living.

What is your house's greatest achievement?
The generous, cleverly laid out spaces that mean we
can have a party and the kids can sleep through it.
Also the patterns and textures of the finishes that
have fed our very souls.

What is your most treasured possession?
Everything I own.

What would you rescue if there was a fire?
Back up the truck!

What quality do you admire most in other houses?
A big bathroom. The only thing I would change
about our house is the size of its bathrooms.

What is the most extravagant expense in the house?
The marble floors.

What would you spend your last decorating dollar on?
Wallpaper.

When was the house's lowest depth of misery?
Probably when the original owners died.

Who are you influenced by?
My mother Virginia Gibbes, Tony Duquette and
Marimekko. Ricky Clifton floats my boat in the
design world at the moment.

What's the worst thing your house has ever done?
Let carpet moths get hold of the original carved
wool carpet.

*Do you love or hate Pinterest? Colour coding books?
Butcher tiles?*
I find all of them boring.

Are you decoratively optimistic?
I'm really hoping we are emerging from what seems
to have been an eternity of bog-boring beige and
murder by minimalism.

*Do you ever pinch yourself when you look around,
or did you always know you would end up in a house
of pure beauty?*
I have total gratitude on a daily basis.

*Do you sometimes sing 'Bisou Bisou' to Drew at night over
a cocktail or has* Mad Men *ruined your domestic life?*
We were sipping on cumquat crustas with me in
a patio outfit well before *Mad Men* graced our
screens, but we are so glad it did.

*Is suburbia worth it for a joyous backyard and
an Alice Brady kitchen?*
Not forever and ever.

*Who made the lovely silhouettes of your girls in
the lounge room?*
I did! And with great difficulty! I cut the cardboard
by hand with a scalpel, working from a photocopy
of their lovely little heads, then framed it.

What is your mantra?
Be brave. Decorate hard.

daughter

mother

THE

POWERFUL

GIBBES

WOMEN

2

Virginia Gibbes

Portsea

You know how when you arrive at a wedding you can feel its vibe within the first five milliseconds? It's either going to be an obligation-driven clock-watcher or the best night ever. Great atmospheres are amazing. And when they occur naturally in homes they should be savoured.

The air in Virginia Gibbes's beach house carries its own invisible energy. And it's truly all kinds of wonderful. This house is home to Virginia, and her daughters, her son-in-law and her granddaughters on the weekend. It has hosted many a party – in fact, it had to be restumped because all the glasses jumped off the bar when the kids ran down the hall. It's all flair: the kind of flair that you just can't buy or hack together.

This is the kind of place that warrants a full page of star stickers in the diary entry of the day of your visit. It's the kind of place that makes you want to say 'mahalo', even if you've never been to Hawaii. No matter what Virginia handed you from her bar, you would drink it gladly without prejudice.

How did Virginia, originally a Southern belle from Norfolk, Virginia, get to Portsea? She fell in love with Australian aviator Peter Gibbes in Hawaii, straight after World War II. They moved to Melbourne and raised their family. She is now ninety, and the matriarch of an incredibly close family who decamp to her house as often as they can. They play cards, read, cook for one another and swim. Neighbours walk through and the bar is always open.

There is a lot to learn from Virginia's house. The walls are literally held up by the memories of a beautiful life. Her floor-to-ceiling photo wall puts any professionally salon-photographed family gallery to shame. It also makes any designer-driven French hang look like a preschool effort. Hers is the real deal. It's full of love and is possibly the most beautiful thing I have ever seen.

Her vintage Marimekko selections for the guest bedrooms are as vibrant as ever, proving their worth in terms of investment and longevity. Her indoor plants are epic. The fifty-year-old *monstera deliciosa* is more than just a feature, it feels like it actually holds up the wall. 'My best friend planted it when she lived here. Me, I've just been watering it every week for fifty years.'

Finally, her views on being the hostess with the mostest call for major respect. 'No-one has ever starved here, but no-one has ever really come for the food!' laughs Virginia, adding, 'I never wanted a huge kitchen, I wanted to get in and out of it as fast as I could. A great evening is rarely about the food, it is always about the people. The house has been truly loved by all who have lived in it, and all who have visited it.'

You have no say over
most decorative decisions.
The house decides. You reside.

Where are you now?
At Portsea, in the living room. The sunshine is pouring
in and the house is in its winter arrangement.

*Have you always run the house with a winter
and summer arrangement?*
Yes, of course. Doesn't everyone?

What's important to you when it comes to the house?
Congenial family – enough room for all . . .
oh, and writing pens that work.

If your house was a phrase, what would it be?
Home sweet home.

Where in your home are you the happiest?
In bed.

What is the key to a good life?
Family.

*If you could change one thing about the house,
what would it be?*
The recalcitrant shower.

What is your house's greatest achievement?
Lasting so long.

What is your parallel universe house or place?
Hawaii.

What is your most treasured possession?
The lampshade with the picture of me on my husband's
shoulders, surfing at Waikiki beach in 1946.

What would you rescue if there was a fire?
The lampshade.

What is the most extravagant expense in the house?
Grog.

What is the most over-rated real estate virtue?
Huge bathrooms.

Where else have you lived?
Hawaii, and Sri Lanka in the 1940s.

What's the worst thing your house has ever done?
Locked me out.

If your house was a singer, who would it be?
Bing Crosby.

Where will you grow old and what does it look like?
I have already done that and it is a seascape –
mainly smooth, but with occasional rough patches.

*Is your way of life now a response to your
formative years?*
Yes – l felt loved which, luckily for me,
has continued.

What's your greatest domestic skill?
I'm yet to find it!

Is your house male or female?
It's both – it's everything.

What's the one thing you wish everybody knew about?
Creosote stain.

Who floats your boat in the design world?
Caroline Gibbes (see page 82).

Are you decoratively optimistic?
Yes – I can just call Caroline.

What went on in this house back in the day?
Laughter, parties, good times and cleaning fish.

*What is your advice to people who have young
families and are not really having fun – dealing with
head lice, bad kitchen renovations and unaffordable
real estate prices?*
Battle on – try to find the funny side.

What kind of house did you grow up in?
A wooden-shingled house near the water,
school and buddies in Norfolk, Virginia, USA.

*Do you love or hate Pinterest?
Colour coding books? Butcher tiles?*
I don't have a clue what ANY of them are.

COMING

FULL

CIRCLE

Marie Hélène Claudel Gilly

Le Bailliage

It has been said that Marie Hélène Claudel Gilly's family home is the perfect image of French harmony but it is actually more of an interior polyphony. Le Bailliage's exquisite rooms can make you feel punch drunk from their atmosphere. To live in a truly old house means walking a little more softly and treading a little more carefully within its walls. But to live in Le Bailliage is to live amongst the secrets and the spoils of another life altogether.

Le Bailliage is in Chatou, 14 kilometres from Paris and home to the Impressionist movement. Not in a token way – the Seine River is literally where the steamboat chugged past and Renoir's friends sat for their jolly *Luncheon of the Boating Party* at Maison Fournaise. Le Bailliage itself is inextricably linked to this era, its artists and the ghosts of 'Le déjeuner des canotiers'.

With poet Paul Claudel for a grandfather and the sculptress Camille Claudel (once Rodin's mistress) for a great-aunt, art runs in Marie Hélène's veins. The daughter of a diplomat, her early years were spent traversing the globe. She has now returned to Chatou to be with her father in his twilight years. Her father's 104th birthday was held in the garden the day before our shoot, beautiful evidence of this home's role in the circle of life. Its rooms are arranged in enfilade, with floors of stone, beamed ceilings and oeil-de-boeuf windows. This is a house to both convalesce in and celebrate in. It is romantic, but the experience of the house goes deeper than this.

Marie Hélène's gift for entertaining, her devotion to the arts and her genuine love of people makes her house spirited, as well as beautiful. Constant use has kept it young, its impeccable 16th-century proportions have retained its dignity, and scores of appreciative visitors enjoying its effortless hospitality has kept its spirits up. Stories circulate the world over about Le Bailliage's legendary reputation as the ultimate party house.

Once inside, it isn't plausible to call the interiors 'decoration', because that implies a deliberate hand, a menacing designer or money spent. It really is more of an 'atmosphere' that starts at the front door and ends at the back. It's the kind of house where an hour's visit extends well into the evening without you even noticing. It makes you want to go home and start your own space again from scratch, no matter how fond of it you were beforehand. It leaves a deep imprint on your mind about what it is to live so richly and without pretense.

It might also make you question your own home's paint colours. My affection for blue felt garish when I saw the upstairs library. 'It was appropriate to get a French blue close to bleu roi but lighter,' says Marie Hélène of the shade. And what about the dreamy icy lemon on the landing? 'Oh, this was simply to attract the sunlight.'

When asked what her house would be if it were a phrase, Marie Hélène offers a line from Baudelaire's 'L'invitation au voyage'.

Là, tout n'est qu'ordre et beauté

Luxe, calme et volupté.

~~~~~~~~~~~~~~~~~~~~~~~~~~~~~~~~~~~~

There, where all is order and beauty,

Luxury, peace, and pleasure.

— BAUDELAIRE

66

Who lives here?
My 104-year-old father, his Vietnamese carer and me.
We are answering these questions while we have lunch
together in the garden.

If your house was a phrase, what would it be?
Luxe, calme et volupté.

What is your greatest extravagance?
Entertaining.

What is the most over-rated real estate virtue?
Swimming pools and air conditioning.

What is your house's greatest achievement?
To have existed for 350 years.

What is your most treasured possession?
My two dogs.

What would you rescue if there was a fire?
The dogs!

What would you spend your last decorating dollar on?
Beautiful mirrors.

Can you cite three influences?
My mother, my aunt, and the embassies I have lived in.

What do you find beautiful?
French mirrors, Japanese prints, Chinese tables...

If your house were a singer, who would it be?
A baroque concert singer.

Where will you grow old, and what does it look like?
Hopefully I'll be by an ocean, such as the one
in Tangiers.

What was your childhood like?
It was a dream childhood: Brussels, Naples,
Tangiers and New York.

*Is your way of life now a response to your
formative years?*
Yes. I live in my mother's house, which was
decorated by her!

*You have lived here as a baby, a young woman and
now a grandmother. What has this house taught you?*
Elegance is more important than luxury.

How long has your father lived here?
Most recently, he's been here since 1997. And on
and off before that, between diplomatic postings.

Are there any downsides to living in a chateau?
The unexpected expenses and heating bills!

Upsides?
Timeless elegance.

*Do you sense the ghosts of le déjeuner des
canotiers when you go to the shops for milk?*
Yes, they are everywhere.

Can a house make you happy?
Yes.

What is your fondest memory?
The sixtieth wedding anniversary celebration
that my parents held in the garden.

What is the secret to a good, long life?
Moderation. And going for walks with the dogs.

If the walls could talk, what would they say?
They would have so much to say. The French
Revolution, two world wars, and many, many artists...

✳

JON MOSLET & MARCO SCIRÈ

HOW TO HOST

(NO MATTER WHAT YOUR HOUSE IS LIKE!)

Being an effortless entertainer is actually more of a skill than a birthright. It takes nerve, verve (also of the orange-labelled kind!) and a certain level of diplomacy. Not only does Jon and Marco's Sicilian villa, Rocca delle Tre Contrade, have one of Europe's best swimming pools (as voted by Vanity Fair!) but they are also renowned for making everyone they meet feel welcome and comfortable.

ANTICIPATION is key! When inviting guests, whether to an intimate dinner or a big affair, you need to make sure it will be an event to remember. Nothing spurs enthusiasm more than an occasion. It could be as simple as a recent small victory, a belated anniversary or life itself!

The *INVITATION* sets the tone – even when it's digital – and gives your guests something to think about. A request for an RSVP always raises the bar and adds a little additional anticipation.

Don't be overly ambitious in your *PLANNING*. Think through all aspects and make the necessary preparations well in advance. If you aren't sure that everything can be planned well ahead of time, rein in your ambition and simplify – or get helpers. Make a list and delegate.

Don't be afraid to *MIX AND MATCH* your guests. If you get along terrifically with two people, it's likely that they will get along too. Meeting new people enhances the experience for your guests and makes the occasion even more special, worthwhile and memorable.

Incorporate an element of *SURPRISE*. Think back on a recent social, travel or food experiences that blew your mind. Try to recreate even a tiny part of that. A new cocktail recipe (invite the barman who invented it), an exotic ingredient (bring it back from your travels), a sound (invite the musician), a phrase from a book (project it on the wall) or an accessory (give it to everybody to wear).

Consider *PRACTICALITIES*. Everyone looks better in candlelight. Movement keeps the event alive, so make sure seating is sparse (except, of course, around the dining table). Provide enough food and wine (never underestimate). Load up your favourite playlist (and don't let anyone hijack it). A seating plan for the table is always a good idea (put the 'mix and match' into practice).

Don't forget to *RELAX AND MINGLE*. Chat with your guests, make introductions and enjoy what you have created! These events usually find their own trajectory – all you can do is surrender to fate. Your guests will enjoy themselves more if you are able to let things unfold at their own pace.

DOMICILE

Eugenia Lim

Melbourne

'Act As If...' is one of my favourite fixes for life's big questions. Let's play.

Act As If... there is endless money – as much as anyone could possibly ever need for 40 square metres – and a pile of ideas eager to play themselves out in your spacious home and you are ready to bring them all down in a thirty-day window.

Act As If... all the tradespeople you are working with have a telepathic insight into your devoted and unscrambled brain and they know exactly what you are trying to do. Or Act As If... your ground-floor beach apartment is a glorious Jamaican-inspired guesthouse on the coast of Italy ready to cut ties with its previous dowdy 80s owner.

'Act As If...' is a coaching tool that sits closely to the theory of the law of attraction and is basis of many positive hypnosis approaches. (I enjoyed the totally unrelated Harvard basketball coach Kathy Delaney-Smith's movie *Act As If*, just in case you are a mad basketball and interior lover too.)

So let's Act As If... the world has a shared belief in small footprint living. And that it is possible to both add to the built world but also improve it. And that a small family and an art practice can be a successful plan.

This is the work that artist and editor Eugenia Lim has been setting up and doing for most of her adult life, first through Assemble Papers and now with her own solo art practice. She lives with architect Quino Holland, their toddler Ida and Chips the greyhound in a Victorian worker's cottage and their set-up is best described as high-grade. Compromising on nothing when it comes to quality – from food to work – they have chosen to live in an area where they are part of a genuine community. They choose to do a handful of things as best they can, rather than take on everything that falls into their self-employed laps. Eugenia works from a studio nearby.

Act As If... work is important and the outcomes will be: 'Having an active kid means I have to work fast. There is no time for procrastination so the studio is a calm oasis where I can think and work.' Act As If... nothing is set in stone: 'I need to constantly take a step back from the daily grind sometimes to see what is working and what needs shifting.' Act As If... it's your last meal: 'Cooking is my absolute joy and we take our simple meals with ridiculous amounts of pleasure in our house!' Act As If... your inspiration is your guiding light: 'I gather a lot of strength from investigating Xavier Corberó's incredible home. It's an ever-evolving, never-finished artwork of exquisite beauty.'

Eugenia makes every part of her life mindful and art-filled and the results are beyond the picture of her astute decorative resolve. The great Charles Eames said, 'Eventually everything connects – people, ideas, objects. The quality of the connections is the key to quality per se'. Maybe we should all take Eames's words as gospel or at least 'Act As If'.

Your house is not
a performer. It should be
itself every time you
walk in the door.

What is your house's greatest achievement?
Remaining vertical for so long.

Who are you influenced by?
I only need one – the art of Sophie Calle.

What's on your bedside table?
Ghost Cities of China by Wade Shepard.

If your house was a singer, who would it be?
Beth Gibbons from Portishead.

What was your childhood like?
Messy but uptight.

Do you have a great domestic skill?
Yes, making coffee.

Is your house male or female?
Most definitely female.

*When we met I was taken aback at your decorative
resolve. Can you tell us a bit about your approach
to work life and home life?*
My work space tends to be the messiest. I work a lot
with gold emergency blankets and they cover most of
the surfaces in the studio! At home, past artworks of
mine and the works of friends cover the walls in a jam-
packed salon-style hang. Home is a bit of a battlefield
between the clean minimalism and purity of the
architect and the chaos of art.

*How did bringing a small human into the world
affect your work and home atmospheres?*
Less time, more chaos, more fun, more focus. It also
forced me to move my art practice out of the kitchen
and back into a dedicated studio. At home it is always
loud and there is a constant layer of food scraps on
every surface.

What you would do differently in either space?
I'd like more storage in my studio, better insulation
(it's officially freezing in there in winter!) and more
room for filming and prototyping. At home, I'd like
more open-plan space and a kitchen that looks onto
the garden for maximum toddler-observation with
minimal effort so I can cook while Ida does burnouts
in the garden.

*Did your large dog have to be trained to come to
grips with sharing her home with your daughter?*
No, Chips was cool with Ida. Chips is a bit of an ice
queen with children but she's coming around to the
idea of a 'sibling'. She was and is very tolerant of ear
and tail pulling! Greyhounds tend to be very gentle and
good with kids, so no therapy or training was needed.

*What are your tips for living with a dog
and a small child?*
You will need to deal with lots of poo.

What is your idea of perfect home happiness?
Order in chaos. Being surrounded by art and books.
Fresh food in the fridge or, better yet, a Le Creuset
pot of delicious leftovers!

Which living person do you most admire?
Agnès Varda.

What is your greatest extravagance?
My book and magazine addiction.

What is your home's greatest extravagance?
She's pretty modest really. Maybe our Rega turntable
that we don't spin much to save it from the sticky
fingers of our toddler.

If your house was a phrase, what would it be?
The magnetic field between art and architecture.

What is the most over-rated real estate virtue?
Size!

*

J. J. MARTIN

HOW TO MAX OUT

No one understands maximalism more than my friend J.J. Martin, fashion journalist and editor of Wallpaper*. *From her Milan studio, she shows the world that being a maximalist takes more than a slap-dash approach. It requires rigour, planning and a fine balance – because nobody wants to be stuck in guck!*

NEVER, EVER BE AFRAID TO MIX DIFFERENT PRINTS

Patterns that seem disparate often sing when placed together. The trick is to follow one line of thought in your pattern clashing – a shared colour palette, for example, works wonders. I love balancing feminine blooms with something more rigorous or academic, like geometric prints or bold stripes.

CHAOS ALWAYS REQUIRES BALANCE SOMEWHERE

I love to think of my interiors as raucously printed and boldly hued, but the lines of the house have to be clean and rigorous to contain all of that mayhem. Otherwise you're stuck in guck.

PAIR THE UNEXPECTED

My favorite balance is Nordic or Rationalist architectural lines – fluff-free, very pure, no embellishments – paired with exuberant Italian flourishes in the textiles and furniture pieces.

MAXIMALIST WALLS CAN BE ACHIEVED IN MANY WAYS

Think of bright paint scattered with archipelagos of framed artwork, your favorite upholstery fabric used as wallpaper with clashing paintings hung over it, and wallpaper that matches the bedspreads or couches (which I am a total sucker for).

KEEP YOUR KNICK-KNACKS TO A MINIMUM

Whoever you are living with never wants to see them as much as you do. If they must appear, cluster them together into small artful collections.

QUEEN

OF

HEARTS

Nikki Tibbles

London

There are two things that make Nikki Tibbles happy – flowers and dogs. This is how it has always been but now her two passions overlap at home and at work.

Nikki first made a name for herself with her Wild at Heart flower studio, dealing generous dogwood, ranunculi and peonies to London's English roses. Her other accomplishment, Wild at Heart Foundation and its fearless work with dog rescue, has won her even more praise.

Both Wild at Hearts meld together gloriously in her Notting Hill townhouse where the dogs are many and the vases are always full. When I visit, five live-in rescue dogs (Reuben, Tia, Lenny, Smith and Ronnie) are settled on their sofas and two others (Gina and Mischa – I have my fingers and toes crossed for these guys) are in the process of being rehomed. Thousands more are waiting on adoption.

How did Nikki achieve that ever-elusive layer that reveals a house's true content and undertake a full renovation? Physical and financial exhaustion usually take their toll before the real layering begins. Nikki has managed to achieve what I call the HTH – Holy Trinity House – spatially, decoratively and personally flawless. Every room has her fairy dust.* Every corner is snug, with not a detail spared. Let's go beyond the 'Botanical Trend' of bringing the outdoors inside, and take a forensic look at some of her triumphs.

Despite the obvious parallels to her favourite flower, the garden rose, the inspiration for her living room's perfect pink walls was the setting sun. 'I wanted to see if we could capture it,' said Nikki, 'and I think we did.' Oh, our Father, who art in heaven – she so did. And you can too, with Plaster V by Paint and Paper Library.

Nikki looks high and low, and knows that value is not always determined by a price tag. Hallelujah, and hell yeah! 'I have things I have picked up for 5 euros in a flea market, and a Venini vase that I'd wanted for ever,' she says. 'I also set up a payment plan with Lamberty Antiques for my Paul Evan's glass dining room table!'

She knows her formula works, and she uses it both with flowers and her approach to her home. Working with two or three dominant shades puts her on an instinctive, never-questioning-herself starting block and is second nature to her. This gives her work and home a round-the-clock jubilance that is always harmonious.

Nikki also knows how to put the 'I' into Impact. 'If you are going to make a statement, you might as well be bold,' she says of the Ellie Cashman floral wallpaper she sourced from Instagram. And then, to make it truly her own, she wall-mounted a whole family of limited edition Thomas Eyck porcelain insects on it. As you do.

She has a narrow focus that comes with provisos. This is what stops her collection from looking like a junk shop. 'I collect vases – mostly Fulham – and the only prerequisite is that they have to look good without flowers in them.'

The real revelation, though, is the joy and energy created by a home populated by more dogs than humans. The author Milan Kundera said that dogs are our link to Paradise, which makes Nikki's house a nirvana.

When everything in
a room is all standard
and survivalist – BAM! –
add the visual equivalent
of a Céline handbag.
Sit back. Your job
is done.

Everyone is scared
of their house; that's
why we want rules.
Apply the rules to the space.
Then burn the rule book.

Who lives here?
Me and my five rescue dogs.

What is your house's greatest fear?
Emptiness.

Which living person do you most admire?
Marc Ching, the founder of the Animal Hope
& Wellness Foundation.

What is your greatest extravagance?
Charity – I would give everything I own away.

What is your home's greatest extravagance?
My giant sofa from Living Divani for me and five dogs.

What quality do you most like in a room?
Light, floor-to-ceiling windows and the ability
to get outside to the terrace or garden.

If your house was a phrase what would it be?
Have courage … be kind.

What is your idea of perfect home happiness?
I fill my house with everything I love – my collections,
paintings, wonderful friends and family, delicious food
and, of course, my beautiful rescue dogs – all these
things keep me truly happy.

What do you consider your house's greatest achievement?
Being welcoming to one and all.

What do you find beautiful?
Nature to me is the most beautiful thing. Seeing the
seasons change truly inspires me and offers new ideas
for creations, weddings and events. Also kindness,
compassion and gentleness.

Where will you grow old and what does it look like?
In the middle of nowhere in a giant country house,
with 100 acres and surrounded by rescue animals …
pigs, dogs, donkeys and adopted children.

What was your childhood like?
Warm and happy. My father was just the kindest man,
who loved animals and taught me I could do anything
if I wanted to.

*Who is floating your boat at the moment in the
design world?*
Audrey Carden and Eleanora Cunietti.

What are your tips for a dog-safe house?
I don't really dog-proof my house. I am blessed
with fantastic dogs that have honestly never broken
anything in my home, which is astounding considering
the number of artworks and vases I have on display.
However, I have created a beautifully secure garden,
complete with toy box!

What are the ideal surfaces for doggy paws?
Instead of opting for carpets, create texture in your
house by using wood and stone flag floors. They will
wipe down easily when the inevitable spillages occur.

Are the dogs in bed with you all night?
Or just for cuddles?
All night.

Where in your house are you the happiest?
Either cooking in my kitchen, reading in my
bedroom or sitting in front of a fire.

What is on your bedside table?
Scented candles, vegetarian cookery books
and hand cream.

If your house was a singer, who would it be?
Beyonce!!!

*What staggering fact should we all know
about dog rehoming?*
There are so many facts that I could reel off but,
to put the issue into perspective, three-quarters of
the world's dogs are strays. That is 600 million dogs
worldwide and the problem is only getting worse.

How did the Wild at Heart Foundation start?
I've had rescue dogs ever since I was a child and my
love for animals has only increased with time. Starting
a canine charity has been a long-term goal for me.
I am so blessed to have met Nadine Kayser. Along
with our amazing team, we have grown the Wild at
Heart Foundation together. We want to end the killing
of stray dogs around the world. We aim to do this by
managing dog populations humanely, which includes
reducing uncontrolled breeding and supporting
rehoming and education projects.

Can having a dog reduce your heating bills?
Of course, they keep you warm at night.

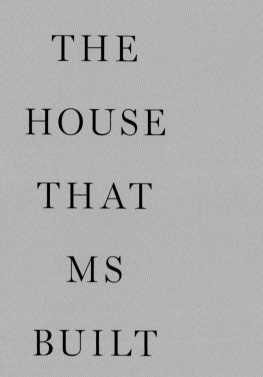

THE
HOUSE
THAT
MS
BUILT

Emma Maher / Hannah Tribe

Sydney

— EMMA

— HUSBAND

— SON

— DOG

Some architects are worth the fanfare. I believe Hannah Tribe is one of them. She makes people want to live in her version of a house instead of losing their marbles over mantelpieces that make them feel like 18th-century Dutch royalty while, in real life, they are sorting the clothes basket.

I am talking about myself here. I almost got a Hannah Tribe house, but I lost focus. I frittered away my renovation savings on things like that imaginary mantelpiece. But I know a lot of people who kept their eyes on the prize and are the lucky recipients of what ex-painter Hannah describes as her 'non-figurative portraiture'.

Emma Maher is one of the lucky ducks. But Hannah reckons she is the lucky one. 'The house for Emma, Ritchie, their son Louis and Molly the dog is one of my office's proudest achievements. Emma wanted a house that had very specific mobility needs. She is a former *Belle* magazine staffer, has immaculate taste and is very interested in interiors. Emma feels her space. You know how some people are spatially sensitive? She is super spatially sensitive. Emma is in a wheelchair most of the time but it was imperative that house not look disabled-y. We worked with Emma's occupational therapist and physio so that the design of the house could support her mobility and independence.'

While Hannah's work is a lot about reduction and dematerialisation, it speaks universally to those of us who remember drawing our dream houses as children. A triangular roof line, a set of square windows, the path to the front door, some flowers in the garden, a small dog and a couple of Vs for birds. If you draw the house that Hannah made for Emma,* that is exactly what it looks like, right down to the white petunias at the front and the cute dog.

Inside the house, a series of mini-house shapes make multiple rooms within rooms. This idea of being in a house within a house creates a rich unfolding world for Emma. 'Sunlight streams in and plays around the walls all day,' she says. 'It reflects off the pool and onto the kitchen ceiling, making the most beautiful patterns.'

Upstairs, Hannah's ceiling cut-outs pull the light in and hand it over to double ceilings that spoon each another with a just-wide-enough gap. Although downstairs is where the light show happens, these double diagonal slopes with nothing but glorious air between them is just part of the house's impressive interior. Its street expression is a perfect blunt disguise to hide its internal complexity.

Hannah describes Emma's house architecturally as 'a series of diagrammatic house-sections within a diagrammatic house extrude.' Press clippings from the architectural press are filled with comments like, 'the evidence of humanity in the process of understanding the client's need and unique brief was flawless in execution' and 'we feel this house could set the benchmark in universal design principles in the future'. Emma's neighbours even commented on social media, speaking of its 'street sensitivity' and its 'lovely hooded roof line'. Emma says it best of all, though. 'She made me a world inside.'

Imagine your favourite recipe.
Slowly, one by one, remove the
ingredients, starting with
the least important ones.
How many things can you take
away before it's no longer your
favourite meal? Now think
of your favourite room and
do the same…

"

*What is your idea of perfect
home happiness?*
Emma / Ⓔ: When all of your senses
are in harmony. A scented candle is
burning, you're eating something
delicious, the music is on and you're
in the space you created so it's also
a feast for your eyes.

Hannah / Ⓗ: Making a house
for a family is a huge honour and
privilege. Architecture is ultimately
an expression of optimism. It is a
dream of a future you want. And a
house is the most potent form of
that – it is the dream of your family's
future happiness. For a house to feel
great, several things need to happen.
There needs to be great light. It
needs to be visually and acoustically
pleasing, and these mean different
things for different people. Everyone
needs to feel pride in the creation.
And there needs to be a layering
of good memories in the space –
the planning of it, the construction,
the moving in, the laughter.

What is your house's greatest fear?
Ⓔ: It hasn't appeared yet.

*Which living person do you
most admire?*
Ⓔ: Ben Quilty.

What is your greatest extravagance?
Ⓔ: Art!

*What is your home's
greatest extravagance?*
Ⓔ: Huge steel-framed, glass doors
that slide into a cavity, maximising
the natural light.

Ⓗ: For me, the extravagance of
Emma's house is in the volume
and spatial complexity. It seems so
straightforward from the outside,
but the inside unfolds and surprises.

*What is the most over-rated
real estate virtue?*
Ⓔ: People's lack of understanding
about prefabrication. It's evolved so
much in building and has massive
economic, environmental and
design benefits.

Ⓗ: I wish there were a count for
quality . . . like four bedrooms, three
bathrooms, two car parks and
'makes you want to weep with misery'
or 'makes your soul soar'.

*Where in your house are you
the happiest?*
Ⓔ: At the dining room table.

*What is your house's
greatest achievement?*
Ⓔ: As I'm in a wheelchair, there
were a number of practicalities that
couldn't be compromised. Hannah
has ensured the space is functional
and beautiful at the same time.

*What is your parallel universe
house or place?*
Ⓔ: Our garden; it's peaceful.

*What are your most treasured
possessions?*
Ⓔ: My husband and son.

*What quality do you admire
most in other houses?*
Ⓔ: Creating ambience.

*What is the most extravagant
expense in your home?*
Ⓔ: Art.

*What would you spend your
last decorating dollar on?*
Ⓔ: Books.

What do you find beautiful?
Ⓔ: Flowers.

Ⓗ: Human kindness.

What's on your bedside table?
Ⓔ: Books, photos and drawings
by Louis.

Where will you grow old?
Ⓔ: Hopefully here.

What was your childhood like?
Ⓔ: Grand.

What's your greatest domestic skill?
Ⓔ: Cooking.

Is your house male or female?
Ⓔ: The exterior is male and the
interior is female.

*What's one thing you wish
everyone knew?*
Ⓔ: Plywood is a fantastic material to
use. A lot of our joinery is plywood.
It looks warm and provides texture.

*Are you the boss of the house or
is the house the boss of you?*
Ⓔ: We take turns.

*If you could change one thing
about the house, what would it be?*
Ⓔ: Nothing.

*What makes the house so successful
in your eyes?*
Ⓔ: The unexpected use of light.
It's so practical; it addresses all my
needs while still being a beautiful
and robust family home.

*As a former glossy magazine
contributor, what ticks your boxes
when it comes to the ideal interior?*
Ⓔ: I'm loving exposed bricks at the
moment. The bricks we've used on
the exterior have been left exposed
on the interior. They're recycled
from the original house.

*Does it surprise you when people
comment on the design of your
kitchen without realising it's
wheelchair-informed?*
Ⓔ: My brief to Hannah was that
I wanted my disability aids to
blend into the design. I didn't want
the space to scream 'a disabled
person lives here'. I could not be
happier, she's nailed every design
requirement.

✳

ROBYN HOLT

HOW TO
LIVE WITH BOOKS

Robyn has done so much in her life that she's hard to define. She's a stylist, a business management guru, an author and a television presenter. She published Monocle, *was editor-in-chief of* Vogue Living, *worked under Saint Laurent, has been the CEO of huge corporations and showed Russians the real definition of style when she launched* Vogue Russia. *But, more importantly, she is a mad keen reader. You can't keep her away from the printed stuff.*

What is the key
to starting a library at home?

It needs to be both calming and charming.
I starting collecting leather-bound books many decades ago, just because I loved the look of them, and then I started to get interested in collecting certain genres. Classics like Thackeray, then Dickens, then *Punch* magazines, then children's books. My advice is to start in a particular genre, then add until complete.

How did your library come about?

In every country I visited, I would buy books about their heroes and stories – often, early editions. I had so many books. I worked with a wonderful draftsman, George Christo, and designs I had pulled from magazines and photocopied from books. I wanted a room I could dine in while being surrounded by books. I prefer not to see a run of spines, unless you are lucky enough to have 30 or 40 spines that are the same. I use objects and treasures to break them up.*

Why is there so much
Russian literature in your collection?

I lived and worked in Russia for four years in the early 2000s. My husband, who is an actor, was a huge reader of Russian novels and plays. He introduced me to the classics, as well as Chekhov, and it changed my view of Russia forever.

How do books like to be cared for?

The older they are, the more care they need. No sunlight or fluctuations in temperature. I do have some books that need to be repaired and it is getting harder and harder to find great bookbinders. The way I look after my books is to do one shelf a month. I check their condition, dust them, open them, have a look (often I just get lost in them) and check they are all doing okay.

Jackets on or off?

Always on!

Which library inspires you?

The rotunda shape of the Stockholm Public Library is incredible. I also really like the Mitchell Library Reading Room at the State Library of New South Wales. I worked for more than a year on a project for them and I never tired of walking through the reading room.

What is your go-to read?

I cannot go past F. Scott Fitzgerald – the artistic decadence is so emotive.

Which three books
should every bookshelf have?

Through the Looking-Glass, Complete Works of Shakespeare and *To Kill a Mockingbird.*

THERE IS

SOMETHING ABOUT

H

A

N

Y

A

Hanya Yanagihara

New York

It's hard not to totally flip out and fangirl over Hanya Yanagihara. For me, she is the epitome of the feminine divine. Now that I've got that confession out of the way, let's get down to brass interior tacks. Hanya's New York home is intimate, organised and pulsates with her travel-triggered collections.

On her bedside alone there is a small plaster bust of Ho Chi Minh from Saigon, iron opium weights from Laos and Burma, a solid silver cow from Mumbai, an old brass bell from Bhutan, a box in the shape of a kneeling deer from Chiang Mai, a snuffbox made of melted silver coins from Cambodia, a mirror-worked embroidered pouch from Jaipur, an iron head from the Indonesian island of Flores, a Japanese Shōwa era bronze deer and tiny silver containers in the shapes of animals from South-East Asia. It's a hedonistic set up for a small piece of bedside real estate, but a perfect representation of Hanya's appetite for life. It's also a snapshot of the glorious atmosphere she has created within the constraints of a one-bedroom apartment.*

First, let's deal with the most gripping question of all – a glorious pink wall that runs the length of her library and dining wall. 'The practical answer is that the pink is actually a superb neutral,' she says. 'There are certain very bright colours – jadeite green, Majorelle blue, Paraiba tourmaline turquoise, hot pink – that have the unfair reputation of being difficult, but really, they're so self-possessed and so singular that they're able to accommodate almost anything you pair with them. The philosophical answer is that it's an announcement to others, or yourself, of another facet of the self, one that might often go unexpressed or unseen.'

Second, how does she find her books in a library that totals over 12,000 titles? Every book is arranged alphabetically by author.

And finally, how has she managed to make the space so incredibly potent? 'The apartment has offered me protection from a city about which I have ambivalent feelings, and it's given me a stimulating place to work,' she says. Clearly the apartment loves her back.

Anyone familiar with Hanya's writing (new readers be warned: she will keep you up all night) knows of her glorious intellect and the shortlisting for the Man Booker Prize. But I have never known a more perfect decorative love letter to living with books than Hanya's reading/dining room. Oh, Hanya!

Ignore the mania for
the new; nothing beautiful
has ever come out of a trend
report. (Everything popular
is wrong, anyway.)

Who lives here?
Just me.

*How long did it take you to answer
these questions?*
Forever, and across many countries
and places: Hawaii to Denmark to
New York to Morocco to Spain!

*Where in your home are you
the happiest?*
At my desk, writing.

*Which living person do you
most admire?*
Rei Kawakubo.

What is your greatest extravagance?
Travelling the way I want to travel.

*What is your home's greatest
extravagance?*
The hinoki soaking tub. I think it's
the single most expensive piece of
architecture in the apartment. It's
a highly mould-resistant cedar and
my architect also lined the walls of
the bathroom with it, like a humidor.
When the water in the bath is hot,
the place is redolent of wood.

*What is the most over-rated real
estate virtue?*
Sunlight (it damages the art).

*Is your home lying or covering
up anything?*
It's terrifically dusty.

*What quality do you like most
in a room?*
Idiosyncrasy.

*If you could change one thing about
your home, what would it be?*
I would've covered it with wallpaper
by Josef Frank and Amrapali by
Designers Guild.

*What is your parallel universe
house or place?*
Takei Nabeshima's Ring House
and Junzo Yoshimura's Summer
House in Karuizawa, Japan; Rudolf
Nureyev's Li Galli islands off the
Amalfi Coast; Donald Judd's house
on Spring Street, New York; the
Dia:Beacon museum in New York;
Rajmahal Palace and Bar Palladio
in Jaipur, India; Liljestrand House
in Honolulu; the Sanjusangendo
temple in Kyoto; Helga's Folly in
Kandy, Sri Lanka; Amanfayun
in Hangzhou, China; and the
Ett Hem hotel in Stockholm.

*What is your most
treasured possession?*
Bass Strait by Hiroshi Sugimoto.

*What is your home's lowest
depth of misery?*
House guests.

*What qualities do you most value
in other houses?*
Eclecticism, self assurance, and the
confidence to make mistakes. I also
love a little vulgarity and kitsch;
I always value a space that reflects
who the owner thinks she is,
not who she thinks she should be.

*Can you describe your
home in one word?*
Inimitable.

*What would you spend your
last decorating dollar on?*
Textiles.

Who influences you?
Elsa Schiaparelli, Kengo Kuma,
Diane Arbus, Shomei Tomatsu,
Peter Hujar, Toshiko Takaezu,
Sue Williams and Rei Kawakubo.

What do you find beautiful?
Anything in which you can see the
artist's hand or the artist's mind.

*If your house was a singer,
who would it be?*
The offspring of Charles Trenet
and Grace Jones.

What is your greatest domestic skill?
Folding things: laundry, paper,
disjointed kites.

*Is your house a summer house
or a winter house?*
Winter.

Is your house male or female?
I think it's MTF.

*What's one thing you wish
everyone knew?*
That painting a space a rich colour
makes any room appear immediately
more intimate (and its owner
immediately more interesting). That
when you don't have art, you can still
hang interesting wallpaper. That you
should never match your artwork to
your design or arrange your books by
colour: interior design should yield
to art, not the other way. I find it
disrespectful.

*What books do you want to
read over and over again?*
The Untouchable by John Banville,
The Remains of the Day by Kazuo
Ishiguro and *Seven Japanese Tales*
by Junichiro Tanizaki.

G E N E T I C

G I F T S

Mandy & Mike Munro

Melbourne

Before he turned to poetry, Walt Whitman was a nurse, as were Tina Turner and Melbourne fashion designer Lisa Gorman. Mandy Munro should also be added to this list of trained nurses who are also creative geniuses. Mandy has shepherded her entire family into the creative arts and is the matriarch of a family business that unites all their passions and pleasures. 'Nurses are trained to be many things,' she says. 'We just have to realise it.'

Mandy manages Tractor Home, a wholesale business that supplies beautiful items, mainly handcrafted in Africa from a diverse range of materials. Mike, a habitual collector who is renowned for his expertise in Australian art and history, is Mandy's number one researcher and buyer. Their daughter Phoebe runs an exquisite retail concern called Pan After, Hamish is a jeweller who has unfair levels of talent in his little finger, and Fergus made a tree change with his young family and is a farmer.

Their house has been the family's home for twenty-five years, but it was only renovated ten years ago. 'We played the long game,' laughs Mandy. It is like a living photo album of their travels (Botswana, India, Greece, Senegal, Peru, Mexico) and, in a time where interior marketing messages are all about 'telling a story', there is nothing in the house or garden that doesn't have a genuine narrative.

Is it Mandy's triage training that keeps everything going, or is the success of the house to do with the energy that is generated by having so many people under the one roof who all appreciate the same things? It is both.

'Mike is always looking and buying. I am always travelling and trading. And the kids are always coming and going,' says Mandy. Do they ever disagree on purchases? 'Yes, but not often. It is usually about the volume of things that Mike comes home with rather than the actual find. I remember him coming home all excited about buying some amazing ceramic plates from an old psychiatric hospital. He had bought hundreds and hundreds of them!'

The couple still sleep on the Rosando bed that Mike bought eighteen years ago. 'We had bought a Rosando sideboard a month or so earlier and Mike spotted the bed. We still have them both but I have to say the bed is the one piece of furniture that we really love.'

Twenty-five years ago, before a renovation was even vaguely on the cards, Mandy and Mike decided to plan and plant their garden. They worked wisely, choosing only things they truly love. The garden is the real feature of the house. It is visible from every room, at every level.

The Munro house has staying power. It made the cover of *House & Garden* back in 1950, but it is just as relevant today. And, a decade after a gruelling PITA renovation (that's nurses' slang for 'pain in the arse'), is there anything they would change? 'More storage in the kitchen,' Mandy says. 'But my laundry is totally brilliant. It is one of my happiest places in the house.' Mike gently reminds her about the benchtop. 'Yes, it's true, I do get hysterical if the stainless steel bench is not clean and shining at all times. That's definitely from my nursing days!'

The less fashion
a house wears,
the more beautiful
it can be.

What is your idea of perfect home happiness?
Perfect home happiness is when the house is tidy
and full of family and friends. This house has been
the family home to our three children, our dearest dog
Dusty, our current dog Google and various other pets
and adopted teenagers over the years – it always been
a very busy household.

Which living person do you most admire?
Yandiswa, one of our crafters from Africa. She lives
under very difficult conditions but still manages to
work as hard as she can and give to those around her.

What can we learn from Africans about life and home?
The African woman is the heart of the home. It doesn't
matter what sort of structure they live in, permanent
or transient, it is always decorated with colour, texture
and love.

What is your house's greatest fear?
That one day an apartment building may be built
next door.

What is your greatest extravagance?
Expensive face cream.

What is your home's greatest extravagance?
I would have to say our exotic and extensive garden.
Mike has designed it but we both spend a lot of time
maintaining it. Roberto Burle Marx, the Brazilian
landscape architect, has definitely been a big
inspiration.

What is the best thing about your house?
The garden is an ever-changing project that will
never be finished.

What would you spend your last decorating dollar on?
I would spend my last dollar on a lamp, preferably
1950s and French!

How do you keep your windows so clean?
Easy, just purchase the correct solution and long-
handled window-cleaning implements and teach your
son how to use them. Once a year we get a professional
clean. It is essential to have clean windows when the
entire house is glass. In winter the sun shines right into
the rooms, but in summer the inside is shaded by the
eaves. It's amazing waking up in this home. I'm not
sure I could live in a home without such light.

What is the most over-rated real estate virtue?
Definitely a double lock-up garage

What's on your bedside table?
A 1950s lamp, two Royal Worcester ceramic statues
(January Girl and Thursday Boy), some bangles
and some books.

What's the worst thing your house has ever done?
Annoy the next-door neighbours.

If your house was a singer, who would it be?
Perry Como or Dean Martin.

Where will you grow old and what does it look like?
Probably here. If not, it would be this house but
with a view of the sea.

What's your greatest domestic skill?
I'm a good cleaner. I run a tight ship.

*Who floats your boat at the moment
in the design world?*
At the moment anything and everything
Alexander Girard.

*Do you love or hate Pinterest? Colour coding books?
Butcher tiles?*
I hate Pinterest, I hate colour coding and butcher tiles
are fine if they are on the wall of the butcher's shop.

Do you have any tips for living with a hoarder?
Mike is not strictly a hoarder as he does sell stuff
and often gives things away. He would say he is
a 'collector'. I do have to restrict what comes home
from time to time, but the trouble is what he finds
is so often amazing.

What is your favourite place to visit?
The Namib Desert.

*What place are you dreaming
of for your next trip?*
Uganda.

✳

SILVIA NOBLE

HOW TO MIX OLD & NEW LIKE A PRO!

As much as we all love to stumble upon that Aladdin's cave of treasure, most of us don't want to live in it. This is what Silvia, dealer of things that help kitchen and hearth, says…

SILVIA SAYS | A rough balance of thirty to forty per cent of vintage pieces amongst everyday and new items keeps the 'musty hoarder crazy lady' accusations at bay.

SILVIA SAYS | Covering smaller collections with glass domes says 'ta dahhh' and keeps dust at bay.

SILVIA SAYS | Don't pop your five Rembrandts and two Monets closely on a wall together. The same goes for an unassuming cupboard with sweet proportions and a fabulous green patina. Place it just like a masterpiece painting, against a dark wall with light directed onto it, showcasing its beauty.

SILVIA SAYS | Prop a small naive painting atop a draped, unassuming cupboard with Spanish moss or a collection of bottles to add another teeny presence, but one that doesn't detract from its inherent irreplaceable character.

SILVIA SAYS | Greenery in a space juxtaposes a fresh edge with the vintage. My go-to easy-care favourites include Spanish moss, air plants and succulents – particularly *Crassula ovata* (Blue Bird) and *Rhipsalis* (mistletoe cactus) with its traipsing, trellising tendrils to strappy stems that are nothing short of sexy, really. Otherwise a thistle, the autumnal colours of a tree branch or rainbow chard from the vegie patch stuffed into the neck of a demijohn does the trick.

SILVIA SAYS | For cleaning brass and copper, flour, vinegar and salt are all you need. One part salt, two parts flour and enough vinegar to form a paste removes years of tarnish and readies a piece to be a polished until it shines. A squirt of hairspray stops any further tarnishing if you want to keep the brass or copper piece just as it is.

SILVIA SAYS | Methylated spirits, 000-grade steel wool, beeswax, rags and disposable gloves will refresh, clean and remove years of grime on wooden pieces. Most old pieces are finished with shellac, which can be dissolved with methylated spirits. Apply with a tiny rub of extra-fine steel wool and remove with a cotton rag (makes sure you wear the gloves, as this is a sticky business) and finish with beeswax.

CABIN FEVER

Michelle Crawford

Huon Valley

— MICHELLE

— HUSBAND   — DOG

— DAUGHTER   — CAT*

— SON   — 12 CHICKENS

Instead of me writing a piece about Michelle Crawford, let's put the kettle on, curl up in a comfy seat and discuss her inspiring tree-change story in a less formal way. We'll let the pictures explain the rest.

then . . .

* One small toddler
* A sweet, semi-detached rental in Sydney
* Armchair gardening
* Walking distance to good coffee and bread
* Dreams of a country life
* Unrealised ambitions of working with food
* Crazy house prices
* An exhausted husband
* Traffic jams
* Bitumen roads
* Wearing high heels

now . . .

* Two pre-teen children
* A weatherboard house in the countryside
* Actual gardening
* Driving distance to good coffee and bread
* Affordable house prices
* Getting stuck behind tractors and cows on dirt roads
* Gumboots
* Land Rovers
* Harvesting
* Chickpea stew in cast iron pots
* Picking blackberries
* Eating tomatoes from the garden in summer
* Fresh milk from a friend's Jersey cow
* Victoria sponge always on offer
* Wood oven outside
* Permanent summer picnic set-ups
* Forty-odd heritage fruit trees
* Writing and styling cookbooks
* Giving away jam
* Potato tortilla (making great use of the eggs when the girls are laying).
* Home fires burning
* Cooking on a wood stove
* Gathering wild mushrooms
* Walking along the river

MICHELLE'S TIPS FOR BREWING A PROPER CUP OF BUILDER'S TEA

*

Good builders are hard to find, so make sure you look after them. Over the ten or so years I've been in this house, I've learnt that a cup of builder's tea offered to the tradies working on your home goes a long way to ensuring an enduring good relationship. Builder's tea is so good that I often make one for myself when I need a 3 pm pick-me-up. Here are my tips for the perfect brew.

*

Nothing but Yorkshire Tea bags are strong enough to motivate builders, who often like a brew that could strip the enamel off your teeth.

Boil the kettle, but don't walk away and leave it to boil too long. Tea needs freshly boiled water. Oxygenated water has a much nicer flavour.

Use a sturdy, fashionable mug that reflects your design aesthetic. We have some lovely Cornishware mugs, or nifty enamel mugs for working outside.

Place one tea bag in your mug. One will usually do, but I've sometimes used two to create the perfect Nigerian Sunset colour that many older builders prefer (think 70-year-old bricklayers).

Hot water always goes in first with builder's tea. Fill the mugs almost to the top. Low tide is to be avoided at all costs.

Add milk to taste. Always full cream, never skim and, for the love of tea, NEVER long-life UHT.

Two sugars are usual, but always ask.

Remove the tea bag before serving.

Offering a good quality dunking biscuit or two will go a long way to getting your project finished on time and on budget. I like McVitie's chocolate digestives myself.

WHAT
GOOD SHALL
I DO THIS
DAY?

Life isn't about finding
  your dream home.
    It's about creating one.

"

Where are you answering these questions?
It is a chilly winter's evening, there is a glass of pinot by my side, our friends have just left after a casual dinner and the children are in bed. I'm sitting by the fire in my favourite leather armchair, with Patch at my feet.

Who lives here?
My husband Leo, our children Elsa and Hugo, Patch the dog, Twiggy the cat and a dozen chickens.

What are your influences?
Nature, *All Creatures Great and Small* and *Downton Abbey*.

What's your greatest domestic skill?
I'll let you guess, but it's not cleaning, sewing or doing the laundry.

Is your house a summer house or a winter house?
Summer. When you fling open the doors and step outside onto the soft green lawn, it's at its very best.

Is your house male or female?
It's an old girl.

Are you the boss of the house or is the house the boss of you?
It's a relationship built on mutual respect.

What is your idea of perfect home happiness?
Holidays, nowhere to go, a house full of friends and delicious things to eat.

What is your house's greatest fear?
Laminex.

Which living person do you most admire?
The Queen.

What is your greatest extravagance?
Cookbooks. I just can't/won't stop buying them.

What is your home's greatest extravagance?
Mrs B (as in Beeton), our Rayburn wood-burning stove. She cost the price of a small car but she cooks our food, heats the hot water and keeps the house cosy. She's more of a member of the family than a stove.

What is the most over-rated real estate virtue?
Ensuites. I don't like to hear my husband's ablutions.

Is your house lying or covering up anything?
She's as solid as the day she was made 100 years ago. We liberated her from fussy soft furnishings, boring carpets and promptly painted everything white (Dulux Lexicon, to be precise).

What quality do you most like in a room?
The windows, and the quality of the light that comes through them. I like a soft light that's not direct.

What is your house's greatest achievement?
Providing a home for our two children to spend their childhood.

What is your parallel universe house or place?
A castle in the Scottish Highlands.

What would you rescue if there was a fire?
At the end of the day, it's all just stuff. Nothing.

What would you spend your last decorating dollar on?
A dark vintage French portrait in oils.

What do you find beautiful?
The outdoors. You'll always find something beautiful in nature; it's one of life's guarantees.

What's the worst thing your house has ever done?
Allowed mice to live in its walls.

TRAVAILLER

ET

JOUER

Olivier Abry

Lyon

'The house has been designed by my wife and me with only two things in mind,' says lighting designer Olivier Abry during our shoot in his heavenly home, a former cinema in Lyon, France. I lean in, keen to know their secret. 'The first is that nothing is to be new, except the kitchen. Everything must be vintage – and I mean heart-stompingly vintage, found in flea markets, eBay or antique stores – and the second is that we can hang art easily, without hammering nails into walls, allowing us to change often.'

Olivier and Françoise have created an interior that really is 'heart-stomping' in its simplicity and beauty. They share it with their adult daughter, Louise, and the family felines and are a magnificent example of successfully living, working and relaxing at close quarters.

A typical work day begins with Olivier's short bike ride to his workshop. He assembles every component of his WO & WÉ lighting range by hand, working with Lyon-based artisans and devoted local suppliers. The care, love and integrity is obvious, but how did Olivier invent a worldwide lighting business after twenty years as an employee of a decoration store?

In a world of big-name designers and social media madness, WO & WÉ lights cut through with quietness in a market that thrives on loud. Despite obvious muses such as Serge Mouille, Jean Prouvé, Achille Castiglioni and O.C. White, Olivier credits a sales director at his former job with planting the seed. 'He kept repeating, "The right product, at the right place, at the right price, at the right time",' Olivier remembers. 'I just feel lucky that it is the right time for me and WO & WÉ.'

It helps that the loosely curated compositions and tableaus in his workshop and his home are the perfect companions to his range. They highlight his gaggle of articulated arms, sensitively toned underskins and weightless counterpoints. It also helps that his never-ending curatorial process keeps both spaces moving and changing.

Olivier unashamedly puts chairs in storage and keeps his interior landscape fresh. 'I don't ever want to tire of them. I am constantly buying chairs or trying to, so it makes sense to rotate them around the house and workshop. This way I am so pleased to see them and the rooms are never left static.' With an enviable chair collection spread over both properties, is there any other chair he would spend his last decorating dollar on? 'A pair of easy chairs by Pierre Jeanette,' he says without hesitation.

In a time when interiors are over-filled and seem to be ticking off token criteria, Olivier's dedication to simpler settings in contained spaces that showcase his love of the design greats stands out. So, for those of us wanting to achieve his interior nirvana, what does he believe is the best quality in a room? 'A room is at its best when it is not overly lit.' Amen to that.

The world is suffering
luxury fatigue.
Get your house
off the meds.

Resting is as
  important as working.

"

Where are you answering these questions?
I'm at home, sitting on my Jean Prouvé chair in front of my computer. It's 7 pm.

What is your idea of perfect home happiness?
Lying on my sofa with a coffee and a book (maybe a contemporary art exhibition catalogue) and some vinyl on my record player.

What is your house's greatest fear?
That I will leave it!

Which living person do you most admire?
Patti Smith.

What is your greatest extravagance?
Making lamps!

What do you consider the most over-rated real estate virtue?
An indoor glass roof (not one by Flore, more like a greenhouse).

Is your house lying or covering up anything?
No, not to my knowledge.

If your house was a phrase, what would it be?
'Less is more'. In my work I seem to achieve it, and in my own house I try…

If you could change one thing about the house, what would it be?
The garden (because I don't have one… and I would love to).

What is your house's greatest achievement?
The fact that I don't get tired of it.

What is your parallel universe house or place?
Le Cabanon by Le Corbusier.

What do you find beautiful?
The Villa Noailles by Robert Mallet-Stevens.

What's on your bedside table?
A pile of novels

What's the worst thing that has ever happened to your house?
A flood.

If your house was a singer, who would it be?
Bryan Ferry.

Where will you grow old and what does it look like?
Île de Ré (a small island on the French Atlantic coast).

What was your childhood like?
Awesome!

Is your way of life now a response to your formative years?
Absolutely.

Is your house a summer house or a winter house?
A winter house.

Is your house male or female?
Male.

What's one design idea you wish everyone knew?
Nothing. A house is best discovered without information.

Are you the boss of the house or is the house the boss of you?
I am the boss!

Who floats your boat at the moment in the design world?
Pierre Yovanovitch.

Do you love or hate Pinterest? Colour coding books? Butcher tiles?
I hate Pinterest and colour coding books. I love butcher tiles.

How do you combine work and life?
I make lamps in my workshop and I work on my computer at home, and I live in my home… we do get along very well, my studio, my house and I.

✳

NINA PROVAN

HOW TO CREATE A KNOCK-OUT PALETTE

Sometimes a double or triple colour combination is a freakish interior accident, but other times it's a deliberate stroke, tenderly delivered. Interior designer and stylist Nina Provan has a sixth sense for colour and a gentle hand. That's why I asked her for a few simple pointers on how to work yourself up in a lather of straight-to-the-heart contemporary colours.

Tell us about the colours at work in this scheme.

I was conscious that a bright bold colour would highlight the smaller size of the apartment. Instead, I chose a soft blue-green called Dulux Moncur, which was painted on the sliding door to the study and the curved nib wall. When I saw Esther Stewart's artwork, I fell in love with the boldness, the geometry and the confidence in her choice of colours. It was the perfect partner to the subtle pastel blue-green on the walls. They each have their place in the space without any competition!

ଉଉଉଉଉଉ

What was the inspiration?

The inspiration came from the curved line of roof in this compact inner-city apartment, which is such a rare feature. It was all about finding a colour that was going to softly accentuate this and hug the curve, rather than being the centre of attention! Then it was about injecting colourful energy into the space through the furniture, artwork and styling. The pink chair is a real stand-out in the living room. I suppose that's where I wanted to make a lasting impression – after all, who could forget a pink chair?

ଉଉଉଉଉଉ

Why do you think people get colours so very wrong?

I think it's because they think they need to follow a colour trend or colour forecast. I don't really subscribe to that, but I do think they can be a great source of inspiration. Trends can encourage you to use colours that you might not have the confidence to play with otherwise.

BRUTALLY
BEAUTIFUL

Fiona Lynch

Melbourne

How's this for an interior designer's total dreamscape: a walk-in client with the keys to an old boot factory that was renovated with a Russian constructivist floor plan and a double-height glass atrium. Sounds bizarre but, hey, crazier things have happened.

When the walk-in introduced himself to Fiona Lynch, she misheard him and thought he said he was a pastor, not a pastoralist. Maybe it was his Kiwi accent, or maybe Fiona just has better eyes than ears. While she is now a highly awarded interior designer, Fiona originally studied fine art and exhibited her paintings (collecting many red dots). Her rooms have her formative artist training to thank and this gives her work a distinct advantage.

This is most evident in the rooms she created for the appreciative farmer, whose hobbies include extreme sports, climbing Everest and swimming with sharks. Heavy-handed shades in monastic materials bounce right up against the building's brutal 70s architecture and bring the attention back to the internals, rather than the architectural gestures. On paper, her choices could look sombre and like bachelor pad clichés, but they are the perfect solution to a series of small rooms that are cinematically lit by the atrium's sun trap.

The farmer's house is one of those double-dip places. It wraps the first-time visitor up in its contained drama and top-line beauty. But Fiona's painstakingly detailed efforts and the incredible level of built details shrink the space down to a unique experience. Which is exactly her intention: 'Painterly, precise and detailed,' she says.

Then there are efforts that only the farmer could ever inform and that only someone like Fiona could pick up on and deliver. Such as the bookcases that are staggered up the height of two floors like a metaphor for Mont Blanc. Or the bush-hammered concrete flooring and the oxidised brass range hood that represents a glowing morning sun.

My favourite detail is the kitchen column that sits smack bang next to a black marble island bench partially wrapped in rubber cord. A personal ode to Alvar Aalto's Villa Mairea, it draws the eye down and hints that there are small surprises everywhere. It has been expertly created by Fiona's painterly hand using hard materials. This reminds me of something fellow designer Rose Tarlow once said: 'In a painting, even the slightest brushstroke can have the power to change awkwardness into perfection.' Even more so when your canvas is a building.

What item do you love most?
Fiona / Ⓕ: The new curved walls in the entry,
which are finished in polished plaster.

Client / Ⓒ: The granite bench top. When I walk past,
I always look at the quartz in it and rub my hands
across the rough texture.

What item were you unsure about?
Ⓕ: Blinds on the angle in the bedroom on existing
angled windows! But they look great.

Ⓒ: The powder room design, but it turned out to be
one of the best features of the house. I actually love it.

What is the most satisfying element in the house?
Ⓕ: The low marble shelf that runs from the entry
to the dining area.

Ⓒ: The library.

Would you change anything?
Ⓕ: The existing oatmeal paint behind the
Boston Ivy in the courtyard.

Ⓒ: Not a thing.

What do farmers and designers have in common?
Ⓕ: A passion for authentic materials and spaces.

Ⓒ: What Fiona said!

Who lives here?
Ⓒ: My middle son Jason and me.

What is your house's greatest fear?
Ⓒ: Beige.

What is your greatest extravagance?
Ⓒ: Travel and watches.

*If you could change one thing about the house,
what would it be?*
Ⓒ: While I love my fish pond I can't help
but think about a swimming pool.

What is your house's greatest achievement?
Ⓒ: It makes me look forward to getting home.
I actually miss it.

What is your most treasured possession?
Ⓒ: A painting of my great-great-great-great-
great-grandfather.

What would you rescue if there was a fire?
Ⓒ: My wallet, passport, painting and Ted, my zebra skin.
I backpacked through eight African countries with it,
only to have the Australian border security try to take
it away even though I had all the paperwork.

What is the most extravagant expense in the house?
Ⓒ: Poliform coat hangers!

What would you spend your last decorating dollar on?
Ⓒ: Art and books.

What do you find beautiful?
Ⓒ: The beach and mountains.

What's on your bedside table?
Ⓒ: A photo of my three boys, *Outback* magazine
by RM Williams and lots of autobiographies.

What was your childhood like?
Ⓒ: It was a country childhood which revolved
around school, sports, farm and beach.

What's your greatest domestic skill?
Ⓒ: Vacuuming!

*Are you the boss of the house, or is the house
the boss of you?*
Ⓒ: The house is the boss.

✳

INGRID WEIR

HOW TO MAKE YOUR ART WALL

Ingrid Weir is a designer. She lives between her city house and a rural property in Hill End, New South Wales, and both of her homes contain effortless art walls. Here are Ingrid's top ten tips on making one of your own.

1

Incorporate typography. I have a graphic design background and tend to think of the wall as a page and the pictures as elements, so I always like to have some typography involved.

2

Look in flea markets. Second-hand finds feel contemporary when mixed with other pieces. I always start my walls off with older pieces.

3

A concept adds intrigue – I have one art wall of 'Travel and Adventure'. Nominating a concept will get your wall finished faster.

4

It's always good to have something personal in the mix, like a handmade card or a treasured photo.

5

Plan out the layout before you start. It does help to lay it out on the floor in front of the wall. Annoying but true – it guarantees a better end result.

6

Blu-Tack underneath the bottom of your frames anchors them to the wall.

7

Add drama by running your art wall all the way to the ceiling.

8

Anything that breaks the flat plane of the wall makes it more dynamic. On one of my walls, it's an Italian calendar from the 1960s.

9

A limited colour palette helps bring it together. Blues and sea greens can give a sense of dreamy adventure.

10

Once the wall is finished, I rarely change it. If there is a bench or table underneath I use that to display new elements, bring in flowers or candles, or evoke a seasonal feel.

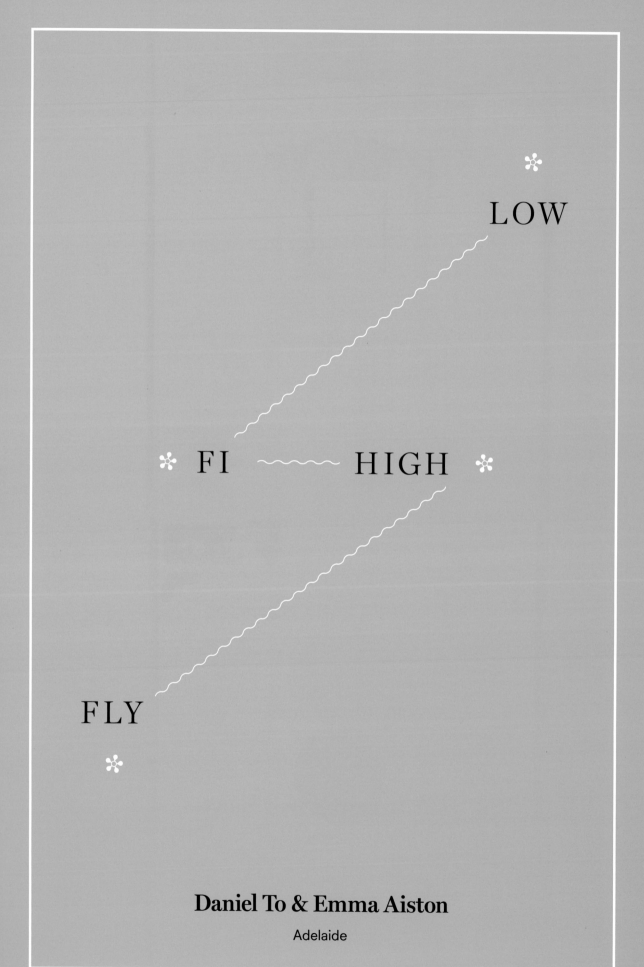

LOW

FI —— HIGH

FLY

Daniel To & Emma Aiston

Adelaide

— DANIEL

— *EMMA*

— DOG

Food, Asia and family* float the boat of Daniel To and Emma Aiston. (It's also why I feel inclined to share Emma's super simple miso eggplant* recipe with you.) The fact that this Adelaide born and bred design duo are international design superstars yet go totally undetected in their Adelaide suburb is just so…well, just so very Daniel and Emma. With the lowest of fi, these two just get on with it.

After spending a couple of glorious days in their company, it is clear that the character space in the DANIEL EMMA logo represents what separates them from other design couples. They share common interests, but have different points of view. They travel the same path, but often reap different rewards. They seem to digest things in the same way, resolve it differently and the split difference is the result.

Problem-solving is a skill they share and a lot of their choices for Dunlee, their 106-year-old cottage, are based around things they just couldn't find, as well as things they didn't need. Daniel and Emma are the only couple I know who endured a renovation without deliberately adding rooms. 'We wanted to be more minimal, so we renovated to reduce, not to add,' says Emma. 'We had a big purge and decluttered. It was very therapeutic!'

The real secret to their design sauce is that they both revel in the usual, working with what most of us overlook to gain their design footing. Take their Cherry on Bottom light, for example. 'It references novelty erasers, most notably the sundae cup with a cherry on the top, and the dye used for our light shade was originally used for making croque-en-bouche,' says Daniel.

'Our stationery container came out of the shape of a light in Daniel's grandparents' Hong Kong apartment,' remembers Emma.

And do the wall hooks take their inspiration from Tic Tacs? 'Yes! But set in solid white oak and mirror-polished bronze,' says Daniel.

Putting aside applause from *Wallpaper**, commissions from Danish furniture design company Hay, and careers that read like a how-to for industrial designers, what is really clear is that Daniel and Emma are opportunists of the best kind. They never overlook the small everyday details and not a day goes by without a great meal. This is how they duck and weave to avoid the high burnout rate in partnerships between designers who are also a couple. 'We try to eat ourselves happy!' says Daniel. In fact, Daniel's birthday party was fancy dress – the only stipulation was that you had to come dressed as food!

And while they have individual views on most things, there are three things they agree on: the Panasonic rice cooker is the one thing they would take if their house was on fire; a cabin in Takamatsu, Japan is their parallel universe; and ugliness is sometimes the most beautiful thing of all.

Cheers to old ugly houses with painted lilac walls and to the young, talented people who choose to improve and inhabit them.

Have you heard
the saying, 'As useless
as the "g" in lasagna'?
Get off Pinterest
and let your
house tell you
what it needs.

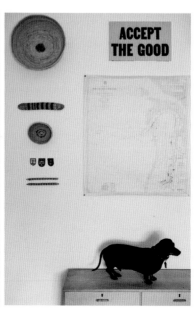

Who lives here?
Us and our sausage dog, Frank.

When you share a business and a home and
a design sensibility, who wears the pants?
Daniel / ⓓ : Always the wife.

What do you both bring to the table,
metaphorically speaking?
ⓓ : I clean the lawn (i.e. rid it of dog poo).

Emma / ⓔ : Everything else (I don't deal with dog poo).

What do you like to do on your summer holidays?
ⓓ : My wife always has great visions for
renovations . . . and I like to keep her happy.

ⓔ : Read a book (or ten).

Where is your happy place?
ⓓ : My only place of freedom is my wardrobe . . .
and the loo.

ⓔ : The ocean or my bed.

What is your house's greatest achievement?
The fact it is still standing after 106 years.

What is your parallel universe house or place?
A tiny cabin in the mountains in Takamatsu, Japan.

What are your most treasured possessions?
Frank and the Panasonic rice cooker.

What do you find beautiful?
Ugliness.

What is the most over-rated real estate virtue?
Home theatre rooms.

What is your house's lowest depth of misery?
The lavender paint that was on every single wall
when we bought it.

What's one thing you wish everyone knew?
That every object has a memory.

What is the most extravagant expense in your house?
Insulation.

What is your greatest fear?
ⓓ : B-I-R-D-S.

ⓔ : Becoming a hoarder.

What is the one thing you wish you had invented?
ⓓ : Fried chicken.

ⓔ : Toast.

Weekends be like . . .
ⓓ : Sunday night sofa and *Family Feud*.

ⓔ : Dancing then lots of sleep-sleep-sleep-sleep-sleep.

What is your favourite spot in your house?
ⓓ : The toilet.

ⓔ : The kitchen. It has superb light all year round.

✳

PAMELA HAYES

HOW TO GIVE A GOOD VILLA

Despite not being part of a five-star chain or having the quintessential Balinese address, Pamela Hayes's property, Villa Sungai, consistently scoops up the awards. Pamela is a self-taught entrepreneur and has trained her local staff impeccably. Villa Sungai is an out of the way plot of jungle paradise, known locally as 'East of Nowhere'. Consider Pamela's lessons if you want to take your own piece of paradise to the next level.

LOVE THY NEIGHBOUR

We took over the riverside land below the houses of the villagers. It was a win–win situation as they were happy to part with it because it was unproductive and it set the tone for what has developed into a wonderful relationship with the village. Most of the older generation had never met westerners so it was a real show of faith, and slowly, slowly we proved ourselves to be good and grateful citizens. Once access ways had been identified it was the time to plant the gardens. I wish I had pictures of the building phase – imagine female builders carting rocks for the foundations on their heads, mostly wearing thongs on the slippery, muddy hillside.

LEARNING | *Consider the unpopular plots and always be nice to your neighbours!*

TAKE IT OUTSIDE

Open-air living is a vital element of Villa Sungai's design. Of course the bedrooms are air-conditioned and totally secure, however, all dining and lounging is done in the open pavilions. In the wet season the overhead fans are necessary, but in 'winter' the temperature is as close to perfect as you could imagine. We also have a range of indoor/outdoor bathroom experiences that fascinate first-timers.

LEARNING | *An outdoor bathroom is about a quarter of the cost of an indoor one. Splurge on one and live it up in summer.*

MAKE A GREAT FIRST IMPRESSION

The welcoming cocktail of vodka, lime juice and palm sugar with kaffir and lemongrass infusions tends to give an indication of what lies ahead! I always remind friends staying with me to remove their shoes as soon as they can, as walking on the cool terrazzo is very relaxing after a long day of travelling.

LEARNING | *No matter what the state of your own plot of paradise, vodka and palm sugar make for a mighty fine welcome.*

VILLA-PERFECT UPKEEP

Expect to refurbish more often than you would at a property where everything is indoors. The most major upkeep we do is to the thatched roof. The alang-alang (type of grass used for the thatching) just screams 'Bali'. Locals don't use it though . . .

We are very grateful to guests who, for the most part, are respectful of their surroundings. The greatest compliment our team gets is that the villas look brand new (despite being built in 1988). We also contract pool specialists, as our pools are crucial to the experience and it frees up our team to focus on guests.

LEARNING | *Clean and deal with scuffs as they come. Also, get yourself a pool man! Saturdays are way too good to be spent at the pool shop asking 101 questions about chemicals!*

THE HOUSE

OF

UNDOING

Caecilia Potter

Melbourne

There are clients who commission interior designers for the good quality stuff (a house that literally hugs you) and those that want to buy a certain energy (a space so sharp only one lounge is permitted). There are others that are after commodified cool (as validated by the likes of *Wallpaper**) and those that want simplicity (reduction, reduction, reduction).

Caecilia Potter is well aware of these categories and appreciates them all. She is only interested in designing spaces that have their own awakening. Her pragmatism, which may come from having trained as a chemical engineer and lawyer and then working in IT, mashes with her design senses. Her work is for people who want houses for themselves, not the houses she might want them to have.

Her own home is full of boys (her husband, their sons and their many friends), and cats. It works around the clock – dinners, parties and drinks are all supported by her generous kitchen garden. It's a stately Victorian mega-terrace that has forgotten its airs and graces. Its intricate detailing has been diverted by Caecilia's high-octane design mix. She specifies super-modern pieces, usually fawned over by minimalists, and force-feeds them into a room full of distant relations to create a glorious, heady atmosphere.

Every room in her house seems to be activated – ready to perform at its highest level, whatever its purpose. Take, for example, her unrelentingly comfortable reading room sofas. The set-up is like a book club in waiting. Her favourite reads are piled high, a table is set for tea and a sound system is ready. Caecilia says this is, 'one of my favourite places to be'. Her art collection is illuminated by LED track lights that are moved when new acquisitions join the wall party, which happens frequently.

The kitchen is commercial in structure but farmhouse in feel. 'My Aga is more of a friend than an oven,' she says. Her dining room's 'ready-set-host' arrangement tempts you to fish for an invitation. (Caecilia? Are you listening?) Positioned to preserve a 110-year old peppercorn tree, her freshwater pool is cleaned using German technology, rocks and plant life. 'It was a challenge, but swimming in living water makes it so worth it.'

I suspect she even measured the length of her arm when positioning the bathtub and its nearby storage. 'I did.'

How does she do it? Zoffany meets Ingo Maurer? Manuel Canovas with Pascal Tarabay? Solar-panelled pergolas and Philippe Starke? Because, in all honesty, if you looked at it on a mood board it might make you feel queasy. 'High contrast,' Caecilia answers. This former 'Queen of the Street' corner mansion has been hit so firmly with the contrast stick you don't even notice she has her own tower* and set of spires as a crown on top. 'Exactly,' agrees Caecilia. 'And it's delicious to live in. You literally move through the house, recharging, resting or revelling in its energy, as you need.'

When designing your living room imagine your visitors thinking, 'I want to sleep with the person who lives here'.

Apply luxury and stealth to
a room even if you're scraping
the coins from the bottom of
your purse. Your efforts will
stand out even more.

66

Who lives here?
It's an ever-changing feast, but currently myself, James, Jasper (21), Cyrus (17) and Bacon the cat.

Do you ever have a nightmare where you go home to a John Pawson-designed cube with a tatami mat and one rail of camel-coloured clothes?
It's funny that you ask that – his interiors and architecture often have an extraordinary monastic quality that I find very appealing! They are beautiful, but I think I would mess them up pretty quickly. But I do actually dream of staying at Pawson's Life House in Wales. That meditation room is sublime, the interiors are truly peaceful and quiet, and the building sits perfectly in those wild surrounds. Truly inspiring – an antidote to my crazy, eclectic world!

What is your house's greatest joy?
Being so flamboyant.

Which living person do you most admire?
In terms of design, Patricia Urquiola for her boundless energy, design flair and her joyful, colourful signature. In life, my dad. He is an Emeritus Professor and, at the ripe old age of ninety-one, he still works about five hours most days, publishing, patenting and commercialising his groundbreaking original research. He also finds time for his seven children and hordes of grandchildren and great grandchildren. He is a a daily inspiration!

What is your greatest extravagance?
French champagne, of course.

What is the most over-rated real estate virtue?
Safe interiors and boring beige! Life is too short not to express yourself and have fun with your home.

What qualities do you most like in a room?
Warmth, friendliness and surprises – the unexpected.

What is your house's greatest threat?
A future buyer who might destroy that patina of age and original features. Although the exterior is heritage-listed, the interior is not.

What do you find beautiful?
Lots of things – beautifully resolved pieces, whether contemporary or antique, but also pieces that convey handmade artisanal values, history or personal meaning and have a sense of integrity that makes them timeless.

What was your childhood like?
Rollicking, in an opinionated family of ten. Full of love.

Is your way of life a response to your formative years?
I've always been used to having lots of people in my home. We welcome visitors and love throwing parties and dinners.

What's your greatest domestic skill?
I absolutely love cooking and I've trained up my elder son, so now he cooks up a storm for us and our friends. What a great retirement plan!

Is your house a summer house or a winter house?
Probably summer, when the garden explodes.

Is your house male or female?
Definitely female. She is an elegant but very warm and friendly old lady who likes hosting parties and is in love with our book collection. I could feel the personality and character of our home the moment I entered it.

Are you the boss of the house, or is the house the boss of you?
When I was a little girl I was determined that the minute I grew up nobody would ever be the boss of me – and that definitely includes the house!

Do you love or hate colour coding books? Butcher tiles?
I abhor colour coding books. It is too anal for me. Butcher tiles are great in the right context but they are currently horribly overused. Except I am totally in love with the new Metro collection by Porcelain Bear. Their curved tiles just blow me away. Especially when they are pieced into marvellous columns and topped and tailed with shark-nosed slabs of divine, expressive marble.

What would you spend your last decorating dollar on?
A dining table – a capacious, lozenge-shaped version of Porcelain Bear's Metro table, custom-made by the two big Bears.

What are your tips for living with kids and cats and also having investment pieces?
If you decide to show your sculptures on low coffee tables, make sure they are really heavy bronzes that little people can't pull over. The heavier the better. And remember that it's far better to enjoy your favourite pieces, even if something occasionally gets chipped or dropped, than to have them stuffed away gathering dust in cupboards!

What is an interior designer duty-bound by?
Honour the site, the architecture, the history and the client's personal story and everything else should follow.

Gemütlichkeit.

In German, it's like saying something is really cosy,
but even better. Full of unconditional love and acceptance.
Although there isn't an English equivalent for this mouthful
of a word, I hope that the places in this book give you
a similar feeling.

�֎

JEAN NEWTON

HOW TO STAY SANE & OUTSMART COCKROACHES

My grandmother is a mighty fine practical woman. Ninety-eight years young,* she has been living independently in her house for the last seventy-eight years. When I asked her permission to share some of her top tips for domestic life, she agreed but 'only if you don't ask me again and I don't have to go on some radio show or anything'.

THE C WORD

Look, it comes down to smarts. Cockroaches detect movement. It's a fact. They only inhabit places that are sedentary. I regularly get my sons and sons-in-law to come over and move my furniture. The cockroaches sense that there is activity and constant movement. I also keep my newspapers and recycling off the ground.

GET YOUR HOSE ON

I refused to spend the whole weekend cleaning all the windows, and I didn't want to spend the money on someone charging me a fortune, so I shut the whole house down and went around and hosed them all with the water on as hard as I could get it. Works very well for people with double-storey houses who don't want to get up on a ladder.

WATER TEMPERATURE

I wash my clothes with lukewarm water only. Never cold or hot – your clothes will perform better if they are cared for this way.

DO YOUR EXERCISES

Take a broomstick to your doonas on the clothes line. It shakes the filling around, revitalises them and can give you some much-needed stress relief. Just hit away!

MENTAL HEALTH

I must say that, after five children, it is safer to aim to get your washing out, dried and back inside in the one swoop. It is better for your mental state to have this done and dusted. Your washing can sometimes represent your mind.

I have lived in the same house for seventy-eight of my ninety-eight years. The key to a happy home is quite simple. You will never have enough of anything: time, money or things. So the only thing you can do to manage your expectations is remind yourself of all the good times. This, and kindness, are key to a happy home life.

*TANGENTS AND RANDOM THREADS

In Minimis Rebus Voluptati
(To find pleasure in small things).

*The polar opposite of Ali's home, Kangaroo Island's
most southwesterly point must be seen to be believed.

*Here's our own model demonstrating
Elsie's Plow Pose.

*When Emma's husband Justin
became obsessed with cycling ten
years ago, she had the neon sign
made for his birthday. 'Ride Me'
is a cycling widow's joke.

*The exterior of the house is a soft
avocado. Anna says, 'the inspiration
for the house's unusual exterior was
the colour of the tree. We love that
it is camouflaged.'

PAGE
⟨ 129 ⟩

*And just when you thought Nikki's house could not get any more covetable, here is her bijoux backyard. English perfection!

PAGE
⟨ 141 ⟩

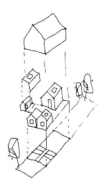

PAGE
⟨ 148 ⟩

*Reading freak Robyn says, 'collecting books is also a lesson in discipline. They really do need care, straight angles, reduced sunlight and constant dusting, but most of all they need to be read, to be loved.'

PAGE
⟨ 84 ⟩

*Does Caroline make the girls read Casa Vogue as well? 'Look, yes and no. I figure it's not going to hurt, right?'

PAGE
⟨ 177 ⟩

PAGE
⟨ 225 ⟩

*Caecilia's tiny tower room and loft sing with Manuel Canovas's tangerine and fuschia paper. Wallpapers reserved for landings, hallways, powder rooms and linings of cupboards are the rockstar way to use it best.

PAGE
⟨ 151 ⟩

*This is a pretty perfect setup for a one bedder in Soho – the curved wooden cocoon bed is just right for a sleeping genius like Hanya.

PAGE
⟨ 211 ⟩

*Daniel To's family portrait – same same but oh so different.

❋

MISO EGGPLANT

Cut 2 large eggplants in half, drizzle with 2 tbs oil and bake at 200°C for 30 minutes or until soft. Mix together 2 heaped tbs miso paste, 1 tbs sugar, 2 tbs mirin, 1 tbs sake and 2 tbs water and pour over eggplant. Bake for another 20 minutes. Remove from oven, sprinkle with chopped spring onions and enjoy with a bowl of steamed rice.

PAGE
⟨ 255 ⟩

*Jean Newtown is my grandmother. I share her with five children, sixteen grandchildren and twenty-three great-grandchildren. She is our Beyoncé and evidence of the house as home, hospice and hope.

P.S.
call your mum

All photography by Brooke Holm
except the following:

Page 1: Suzie Stenmark (Stenmark
Jewels); 6: Eve Wilson; 8: Jenah
Piwanski; 95-105: Jenah Piwanski;
108-115: Pablo Veiga; 116: Phil Huynh;
126: Alberto Zanetti for LaDoubleJ.com;
142-147: Katherine Lu; 188-192:
Pablo Veiga; 195: Eve Wilson; 198-207:
Sharyn Cairns; 208: Ingrid Weir; 220:
Megan Morton; 224-233: Eve Wilson;
234: Aimee Thompson; 236 (left to right):
Steve Lagreca/Shutterstock.com,
Brooke Holm, Aimee Thompson,
Brooke Holm, Brooke Holm, Brooke
Holm; 237 (left to right): Brooke Holm,
Brooke Holm, Hannah Tribe, Brooke
Holm, Brooke Holm, Brooke Holm,
Eve Wilson, Brooke Holm, Aimee
Thompson; 240: Jenah Piwanski;
endpapers: rangizzz/Shutterstock.com.

First published in Australia in 2017
by Thames & Hudson Australia Pty Ltd
11 Central Boulevard Portside Business Park
Port Melbourne Victoria 3207
ABN: 72 004 751 964

www.thameshudson.com.au

ISBN: 978 050050 095 8

National Library of Australia
Cataloguing-in-Publication entry

Creator: Morton, Megan, author.
Title: It's beautiful here / Megan Morton.
ISBN: 9780500500958 (hardback)
Subjects: Interior decoration.
Decorator showhouses.
Decoration and ornament.

Design: Evi O / OetomoNew
Cover: photo by Brooke Holm
Editing: Lorna Hendry
Printed and bound in China by RR Donnelley